Leadership:

EXAMINING THE ELUSIVE

1987 Yearbook
of the
Association for Supervision
and Curriculum
Development

Edited by Linda T. Sheive
and Marian B. Schoenheit

Executive Editor: Ronald S. Brandt
Manager of Publications: Nancy Carter Modrak
Art Director: Al Way

ASCD stock number: 610-87003
ISBN: 0-87120-142-9
Library of Congress
  Catalog Card No.: 86-73014

Price: $13.00

Leadership: Examining the Elusive

Foreword

The guiding concepts for the 1987 ASCD Yearbook are symbolic leadership and culture. *Leadership: Examining the Elusive* challenges us to shape the school culture that teachers, students, and others come to share and, more importantly, that challenges us to behave as guardians of the values, beliefs, and expectations which define that culture. The ability of symbolic leaders to communicate intent and meaning is considered more significant than the behaviors they demonstrate or the events in which they engage.

The ideas and arguments put forth in this yearbook complement strongly the efforts of the Association for Supervision and Curriculum Development to renew emphasis on leadership and supervision as a focus of the Five-Year Plan. This confluence of two heretofore independent efforts is the more fascinating because the content agreed upon so long ago for the yearbook embodies changes in how school leadership is viewed, understood, and practiced and now widely expressed in publications and programs of the Association while urging sustained efforts to look to the future.

It is possible to enjoy and profit from the insights presented by examining the nine chapters as separate entities. But the unusual and diverse aggregate of research, theory, philosophy, and experience become an intricate whole when the examination is guided by a mindscape such as that offered by Sergiovanni. One integrating frame of reference is suggested by the findings of the five-year study by Rutherford from the University of Texas at Austin, referred to by Guild and by Sheive and Schoenheit: vision, goals, climate, monitoring, and intervention. A more familiar mindscape is provided by the five characteristics of instructional leadership drawn from research by ASCD on effective schools and successful corporations. These characteristics have been featured in a videotape and several National Curriculum Study Institutes:

• *Sense of Vision.* To Deal, the "quality of organizations of the future will be those in which leaders have created artful ways to reweave organizational tapestries from old traditions, current realities, and future visions." Owens stresses that "the vision must have some quality that can stir the human consciousness of others and induce their commitment to sharing it as their own purpose." The study by Dwyer, Barnett, and Lee indicates that the key is the presence of effective leadership with vision and determined dedication to make it a practical reality. Much of this satisfaction was related to the effective principal's vision of schools as organizations that promote personal growth and improvement. Guild states that "perhaps the first and most important [aspect of leadership] is the sense of vision, purpose, and mission that the leader holds." Moreover, it is Green's contention that moral problems of educational leaders occur because they lack a clear vision of what their practice is centrally about—to educate.

• *Organizational Development*. Owens points out that the predominant organizational fact about the high school "is the overwhelming influence of the culture of the place in creating organizational structure, establishing coordinated and cooperative effort, and exercising organizational control and discipline." In the study by Dwyer, Barnett, and Lee, other principals directly or indirectly manipulated important elements of the organization while nearly half of the actions by the effective principal were directed toward the work structure of the organization. Champlin speaks of changing the value structure of the school organization and of socializing revised beliefs, attitudes, and relationships into that organization. Even Gabler acknowledges that a "visionary" leader is a type significantly different from the normative school administrator.

• *Instructional Support*. Owens cautions that the "culture of a school is not necessarily, and assuredly not automatically, supportive of education and achievement. It takes skilled, strong, planned leadership to develop the kind of culture that supports high levels of motivation and learning."

• *Monitoring Instruction*. The discussion of classroom visitation by Owens is based upon norms and values established through socialization. The effective principal observed by Dwyer, Barnett, and Lee monitored instruction by regularly dropping into teachers' classrooms. "These visits provided opportunities to make suggestions that did not carry the onus that might accompany recommendations made as the result of formal classroom evaluations." As Green states, the educational leader is simultaneously engaged in shaping the social norms of several memberships; social norms not only form the conscience of membership, they indeed constitute the conscience of membership.

• *Resource Allocation*. Appropriate examples are provided by the principal described by Dwyer, Barnett, and Lee in introducing a set of materials on self-esteem, agreeing to pilot a series for a publisher to obtain needed textbooks, and serving as "linking agent" or "information broker" among teachers. As authors, Sheive and Schoenheit contend that leaders who have evidenced the most success in enacting their vision seem to be masters at identifying resources.

The challenge to the school principals identified by Owens is that they "must be prepared to engage in symbolic leadership and the development of organization cultures of a new and higher order." Moreover, the symbolic educational leader must be a friendly critic of the school culture who creates a new vision of an educationally better culture in the school, and then plans to organize time and energies to communicate that vision to students and teachers alike.

If, as Deal suggests, the time has come to break the cosmic classroom, the culture must be changed. "It is this shared culture of schools and classrooms that gives meaning to the process of education. It is the same stable implicit pattern that frustrates efforts to improve, reform, or change educational forms and practices at all levels." To this, Deal adds that "old practices and other losses need to be buried and commemorated. Meaningless practices and symbols need to be analyzed and vitalized. Emerging visions, dreams, and hopes need to be articulated and celebrated. These are the core tasks that will occupy educational leaders for several years to come."

Reflecting upon the often subtle, sometimes overt discrimination against women administrators in general and women superintendents in particular, Gabler underscores that the underlying problem more often is hidden in the eyes of the beholder than in the skills of the aspirant.

Green warns that "having given us a vision, a glimpse of an alternative context for living and acting with its own resources, its own risks, its own advantages," leaders invite our entrance into that future now. "Leaders without vision, without rootedness, and without imagination are dangerous or at best inept."

Acting on the assumption that the content of the yearbook, significant as it is, is less so than its intent and meaning, it is essential to realize that the journey is more important than the destination, the process more important than the product, and the people more important than the situation.

As Gabler implies and Champlin and the editors state emphatically, the quest is—and will continue to be—worth it.

GERALD R. FIRTH
ASCD President, 1986–87

Part I

ORGANIZATIONAL PERSPECTIVES ON THE WORK OF LEADERS

1

The Culture of Schools

Terrence E. Deal

A l Shanker, head of the American Federation of Teachers, succinctly captured the power of culture in schools and classrooms:

> Ten thousand new teachers each year enter the New York City school system as a
> result of retirement, death, job turnover, and attrition. These new teachers come from
> all over the country. They represent all religions, races, political persuasions, and
> educational institutions. But the amazing thing is that after three weeks in the class-
> room you can't tell them apart from the teachers they replaced.

The classroom embodies a powerful script. The stage, props, actors, and
costumes can vary slightly from level to level, from time to time, or from
place to place. But the key roles and the central drama are almost the same—
even in other cultures. A classroom is a classroom is a classroom. Schools also
show a remarkable consistency across time and national boundaries (Meyer
and Rowan 1983). A recent visit to a high school convinced me that my 20-year
absence from a secondary classroom made little difference. An afternoon in a
Japanese high school several years ago also seemed remarkably familiar. If I
had spoken Japanese, I could easily have taken the place of the teacher whose
class I observed. The campuses of both schools were similar and bore an
uncanny resemblance to those I remember as a student and teacher.

How can we account for the dependability and durability of educational
practices? Despite the number of current theories, no one seems able to
explain why the patterns exist or what we can do to make them different. If
the recent spate of commission reports is accurate, American education is
failing dismally and in fact is in a state of crisis. Has the time come to break the
cosmic classroom? Or do we need to refine or recharge existing practices? In
either case, we need first to understand why the patterns are so stable and
immune to change.

Waller (1932) offered a powerful insight several decades ago:

Schools have a culture that is definitely their own. There are, in the school, complex rituals of personal relationships, a set of folkways, mores, and irrational sanctions, a moral code based upon them. There are games, which are sublimated wars, teams, and an elaborate set of ceremonies concerning them. There are traditions, and traditionalists waging their world-old battle against innovators. There are laws and there is the problem of enforcing them, there is *Sittlichkeit* (p. 103).

Sarason (1971) and Swidler (1979) recently echoed Waller's insights. Swidler noted:

Watching teachers and students in free schools, I become convinced that culture in the sense of symbols, ideologies, and a legitimate language for discussing individual and group obligations provides the crucial substrate on which new organizational forms can be erected. . . . Organizational innovations and cultural change are constantly intertwined, since it is culture that creates the new images of human nature and new symbols with which people can move one another (p. viii).

Two observations from different times, each developed by independent researchers examining very different samples: Waller (1932) looked mainly at traditional schools; Swidler (1979), decades later, studied alternative schools. Their common imagery suggests what the arduous struggle over changing schools and classrooms is really all about. Images of schools and beliefs and assumptions about schooling are encoded early in our experience. The images and beliefs arise from and are tied to a human culture stable over time, largely hidden from conscious view.

In this sense, starting a school from scratch is impossible. Even innovators carry imprints in their heads. Entering any school evokes a predictable script and reciprocal roles. These imprints serve as the basis for educational rituals, the foundation of educational practice. Parents and communities also carry the imprints. The school is a symbol. It needs the right trappings: a flag, a principal, teachers, students, desks, and a curriculum. Those outside assume that those inside are following the script—unless they have reason to believe otherwise (Meyer and Rowan 1983). This shared culture of schools and classrooms gives meaning to the process of education. The same stable implicit pattern frustrates efforts to improve, reform, or change educational forms and practices at all levels.

What Is Culture?

We believe that goals, technical logic, and evaluation govern our modern world. Often, however, they do not. Beneath the façade lurks another world, a primordial place of myths, fairy tales, ceremonies, heroes, and demons—the primitive world that modern ways reputedly left behind. Yet it remains a powerful force behind the scenes in modern organizations. We call them corporations; primitive people called them tribes.

In education, several researchers have tried to conceptualize the elusive symbolic side of schools and classrooms: ethos (Rutter et al. 1979), saga (Clark 1975), and climate (McDill and Rigsby 1973, Halpin and Croft 1962). The concept of culture has also received some attention. Waller (1932), for example, described the school culture:

Teachers have always known that it was not necessary for the students of strange customs to cross the seas to find material. Folklore and myth, tradition, taboo, magic rites, ceremonials of all sorts, collective representations, participation mystique all abound in the front yard of every school, and occasionally they creep upstairs and are incorporated into the more formal portions of school life (p. 103).

Sarason (1971) depicted a similar phenomenon using a different language. He wrote of behavioral regularities and a restricted universe of alternatives. People behave the same in schools and see no real options.

The problem [of change is] inherent in the fact that history and tradition have given rise to roles and relations, to interlocking ideas, practices, values, and expectations that are "givens" not requiring thought or deliberation. These "givens" [like other categories of thought] are far less the products of characteristics of individuals than they are of what we call the culture and its traditions. . . . One of the most difficult problems to recognizing that the major problem in our schools inheres far less in the characteristics of individuals than it does in its culture and system characteristics is that one cannot see culture or systems the way one sees individuals. Culture and systems are not concrete, tangible, and measurable the way individuals are (p. 227–228).

The recent application of culture to modern corporations has spawned still another generation of definitions. Deal and Kennedy (1982) relied on *Webster's*:

. . . the integrated pattern of human behavior that includes thought, speech, action, artifacts, and depends on man's capacity for learning and transmitting knowledge to succeeding generations.

Formal definitions, though verifiable and rigorous, often fail to capture the robustness of a concept as experienced by those who know it firsthand. Culture is an all-encompassing tapestry of meaning. Culture is "the way we do things around here." The ways are transmitted from generation to generation. Culture is learned (Deal and Kennedy 1982). McPherson (1972) illustrated the process of cultural transmission in her intensive observation of rural schools:

Among teachers: "For the old guard teachers, tradition was the key symbol. What I learned in training school or what has always been done. The present is always judged by how it 'used to be done.' Since the past was always far rosier than the present."

Between teacher and students: "To the frequent pupil objection, 'But that's not the way Mrs. Smith did it,' she would respond, 'But you are in fifth grade now. We do it this way' " (p. 56).

Tangible cultural forms embody or represent the ways of a people, or a classroom, or a school:

● *Shared values*—shorthand slogans that summarize deep-seated core values: "IBM Means Service"; "The H-P Way"; "Progress Is Our Most Important Product"; *"Veritas."*

● *Heroes*—the pantheon of individuals who embody or represent core values: Lee Iaccoca, Mary Kay Ashe, John DeLorean, or Angus McDonald, whose efforts to restore service in the blizzard of 1881 are legendary in the Bell System.

● *Rituals*—repetitive behavioral repertoire in which values are experienced directly through implicit signals: the surgical scrub, planning, teaching, the police roll call in *Hill Street Blues*.

● *Ceremonies*—episodic occasions in which the values and heroes are put on display, annointed, and celebrated: the seminars of Mary Kay cosmetics, Hospital Corporation of America's annual meeting, graduation day in schools and universities across the United States.

● *Stories*—concrete examples of values and heroes who triumph by following the culturally prescribed ways: the MacDonald's franchisee who invented the Egg McMuffin and the McD.L.T.; James Burke, chief executive officer of Johnson & Johnson, and how he handled the Tylenol crisis; the principal of the "Magic Mayo" school in Tulsa, Oklahoma, and how she has created an exciting learning environment.

● *Cultural network*—a collection of informal priest/esses, gossips, spies, and storytellers whose primary role is to reinforce and to protect the existing ways: no examples are needed; everyone knows who they are.

Culture as a construct helps explain why classrooms and schools exhibit common and stable patterns across variable conditions. Internally, culture gives meaning to instructional activity and provides a symbolic bridge between action and results. It fuses individual identity with collective destiny. Externally, culture provides the symbolic façade that evokes faith and confidence among outsiders with a stake in education (Meyer and Rowan 1983).

The More Things Change, the More They Stay the Same

Sarason (1971) echoed a phrase that summarizes our experience in trying to change education: The harder we try, the less schools and classrooms seem to change. Several explanations have been offered, each with an accompanying remedy (Bolman and Deal 1984). The most popular explanation focuses on the problem of individual resistance (Baldridge and Deal 1983): Schools are tough to change because professionals lack the required skills and are negatively disposed toward change. To cope with the problem in the past, we have either relied heavily on training or tried to "people proof" innovations.

A second explanation emphasizes the formal structure of schools and classrooms (Corwin 1972, Baldridge and Deal 1983): Changes fail because roles are improperly defined or because adequate levels of interdependence and coordination do not exist. This logic has spawned efforts to redefine roles, to create teams, or to build the problem-solving capacity of schools.

A third explanation evokes the law of the jungle (Baldridge 1975): Desired changes fall short because they threaten the balance of power, create opposing coalitions, and trigger conflict. Political remedies have focused on coopting the opposition, building coalitions to support innovations, or bargaining among warring camps to reach an agreeable compromise or truce.

While each of these perspectives is useful, none adequately pinpoints the key problem of change. Remedies derived from these theories have not altered the modal experience of changing. We still do not fully understand the process of introducing new ways into existing social systems.

Culture and Change: A Basic Contradiction

Looking at the problem of change through a cultural lens, we see an entirely different picture. Culture is a social invention created to give meaning to human endeavor. It provides stability, certainty, and predictability. People fear ambiguity and want assurance that they are in control of their surroundings. Culture imbues life with meaning and through symbols creates a sense of efficacy and control. Change creates existential havoc because it introduces disequilibrium, uncertainty, and makes day-to-day life chaotic and unpredictable. People understandably feel threatened and out of control when their existential pillars become shaky or are taken away.

On an even more basic level, change involves existential loss. (Marris 1974). People become emotionally attached to symbols and rituals, much as they do to lovers, spouses, children, and pets (Deal 1985b). When attachments to people or objects are broken through death or departure, people experience a deep sense of loss and grief. Change creates a similar reaction. A new principal replaces a cherished hero. Mr. Smith, a beloved maverick, leaves teaching for a high-paying position in business. Miss Dove, whose demands and discipline are legendary, takes early retirement because she cannot cope with innovative methods. The computer alters the relationship between teacher and student. Small discussion groups replace classroom lecture and recitation. A graduation ceremony is changed to conform to modern standards. A well-known gossip is transferred to another school, or the popular storyteller suddenly dies.

People develop attachments to values, heroes, rituals, ceremonies, stories, gossips, storytellers, priests, and other cultural players. When change alters or breaks the attachment, meaning is questioned. Often, the change deeply affects those inside the culture as well as those outside. Think of the trauma a school closing or the introduction of the "new math" causes parents. The existential explanation identifies the basic problems of change in educational organizations as cultural transitions.

As a simple illustration, consider the mutual bond that forms between teacher and students:

> As the teacher molded her class and was molded by it, she began to identify herself with it. . . . The original separation of interests, the class as they, as the outgrouping, began to fade away and the formerly imperial rights and obligations become imbued with affect. The teacher, spending six hours a day with her class, began to see the world through its eyes, its interests as her interests, even though she continued to be separated from the pupils because of her authority and the requirement that she must teach, judge, and control them (McPherson 1972, 112–113).

At the end of each school year, the attachment is broken. Both teacher and students experience a loss. Deep-down, the mourning occurs over the summer. Next year's teacher or class will require a transition period before the loss can be repaired. For some, it never is.

Unresolved change and grief either mire people in the past or trap them in the meaningless present. The unhealed wounds following a change can weaken individuals, classrooms, or schools. To heal the wounds and repair ruptured meaning, cultures need to convene transition rituals, to bury and mourn what has been lost, and then to celebrate the new forms that begin to emerge.

In one elementary school in Massachusetts, for example, students held a ceremony and named the corridors after teachers terminated in the wake of cutbacks caused by a taxpayers' revolt. In another Massachusetts school, the faculty convened to pull itself together in the aftermath of the same circumstances. Before the teachers began to discuss the next steps, the principal stepped to the blackboard and asked them to list what the school had lost. The teachers began to list people, programs, and other tangible things that reduced funds had taken away. As the list grew, the tears came. After an emotional hour and a half, the mood of the group began to change. People focused on their emerging strengths—school spirit, top people, adequate facilities. In the transition event, they let go and were ready to move ahead.

Change is difficult because it alters cultural forms that give meaning to schools and classrooms. For change to work, transition rituals are required to transform meaning, to graft new starts onto old roots.

Cultural and Educational Productivity

Corporations across the United States are reexamining and focusing on the culture of the workplace. Culture has become a preoccupation of management because cultural patterns have been conceptually and empirically linked with performance, morale, turnover, image, and other important business concerns (Peters and Waterman 1982, Deal and Kennedy 1982). When some-one at IBM is asked what she does for a living, most likely she would respond confidently, "I work for IBM." She responds that way because her identity is fused with the culture of the company. It is the same in other existentially sound businesses.

Compare the culture of IBM with the culture of schools, an IBMer with a classroom teacher. When teachers are asked what they do for a living, many timidly respond, "I'm just a teacher." Their response may reflect a long-term unraveling of the fabric that gives meaning to the process of learning. Where cultures are cohesive, people contribute their efforts toward a common destiny, rallying around shared values that give meaning to work—and to their lives. When cultures are fragmented, people "do their jobs," worry about salaries, and spend their time struggling for power.

In the field of education, two decades of criticism, desegregation, innova-tion, and frustration have eroded faith and confidence in schools. In the 1960s, researchers claimed that schools did not make a difference (Coleman 1966). The 1960s and 1970s witnessed a barrage of innovations designed to transform education in countless and contradictory ways: new math, alterna-tive schools, management by objectives (MBO). The accountability movement of the 1970s asked educators to provide measurable evidence of learning and mandated rigorous approaches for evaluating people and results. During these decades, schools were asked to solve the problems of the society, but to make their solutions inexpensive. Schools have been soundly criticized for not accomplishing feats that lie outside the ability of the society to perform. These have been turbulent times for educators, and there is no reason to believe that the turbulence will subside in the near future. Witness the new round of criticism and reform.

The real loser in all this turmoil has been the culture of schools. Outsiders lost faith; many professionals have lost confidence in themselves and their practices. What are the shared values of education that various groups can unite behind? If we ask principals, teachers, students, custodians, or parents what a particular school stands for, can they reply, and do their replies create a chorus or a cacophony of individual voices? Who are educa-tional visionaries? Who are the heroes of our schools, and what values do they represent? Are they anointed and celebrated, or are they basically ignored? Who was the last principal or teacher fired for championing a desirable virtue? How meaningful and alive are faculty meetings, parent get-togethers, classrooms, and other cultural rituals? Waller (1932) described the opening exercises of a high school long ago:

> When I was in C____High School, we always began the day with 'opening exercises.' This was the invariable custom, and the daily grind began in every school-room with a few minutes, from a quarter to a half-hour, devoted to singing and pleasant speech-making.

Directly, the last bell had sounded, the principal called us to order by clapping his hands together. There was a last minute scurrying to seats, a hasty completion of whispered conversations. The principal stood on the platform in the front of the room and watched us. His assistant, Miss W., whom we all knew to be the kindliest of souls, but whom we nevertheless feared as if she were the devil herself, stood up behind her desk and regarded us coldly.

When the room was quiet, the principal turned to the music teacher, Miss M., and said, "All right. Go ahead, Miss M."

Miss M. advanced enthusiastically and announced, "We will begin with number 36 in the paper books. That's an old favorite. Now please, let's all sing" (p. 122).

How do schools begin the day now? How memorable and dramatic are opening-day ceremonies, back-to-school nights, graduation, and other cultural ceremonies? What stories do professionals tell each other? What stories circulate in the local community? Many times, the stories about schools are negative, though they should communicate and dramatize the sacred values of education. Consider the following story:

In a large university, a professor was given tenure and promoted to full professor based in large part on an extensive record of publication. It was learned later that many of his publications had been fabricated. The president of the university learned of the fraud and summoned the professor before a schoolwide committee. He announced his decision about the professor's promotion, "You may keep your tenure and your work, but for two years you can have no contact with students. This is the most severe penalty a teacher can receive."

Stories like this one exist in every school and classroom. Why aren't they told? Who are education's storytellers? Where are the educational priests who worry about sacred values and ceremonial occasions?

In business, the connection between culture and performance is commonly accepted. In schools, where the product is complex and intangible, a strong cohesive culture is even more important than in business. The Rutter and others (1979) study of the relationship between school characteristics and productivity identified ethos as a powerful factor in educational performance. In the effective schools research, Deal (1985a) clearly interpreted many of the characteristics related to performance in cultural terms.

Looking beyond the research into the patterns of a typical school, we can see how culture affects performance. Why should students attend class, come on time, or stay in school if they do not identify with its values? How can we expect students to commit themselves to schoolwork when the student subculture rewards popularity, deviance, or athletic prowess? How can a teacher whose loyalties are tied to a union and whose identity is fused mainly with family or another job be expected to put his heart into the classroom? How can he survive the loneliness of teaching without some support from shared values and schoolwide events? How can a new teacher learn the profession without heroes as role models or stories as exemplars? How can a principal shape a culture when her time is tied to complex procedures for observing the classroom? Why should principals spend time walking around or working on values when they are rewarded for the punctuality and appearance of paperwork? Why should parents and community support schools when their recollections of schools are more poignant than their contemporary observations?

One haunting experience in a school summarized the problem for me. I was in a district as an evaluator. My charge was to assess how well new evaluation procedures were working in individual schools. Sitting in one of those small chairs in a 2d-grade classroom, I was interviewing a teacher. I was asking rational questions; she was giving sensible answers. Suddenly, memories of my 2d-grade teacher and classroom flooded my mind. The same sounds, smells, and artifacts. I looked over toward the blackboard, and there it was—the wire chalk holder used to make the music staff. I pulled it across the board to make the five lines. I turned to the teacher and asked her how to make a treble cleff. She quickly jumped to her feet, and I took my chair. It was exactly like my 2d-grade experience.

I said, "That was magic. You must be proud to be a teacher." Her entire posture and expression changed. She talked eloquently about her work and profession for 20 minutes—values, stories, rituals, ceremonies. She was experiencing the culture. I asked her why she hadn't talked to me like that before. "You are from Harvard, and I didn't think you would care about such things," she said. "Why should you? No one here does." I asked her how the evaluation process was linked to the core values of teaching she had just expressed. She said there was no relationship between the criteria and the important aspects of teaching: "I go along to keep them happy."

From this event, I got a sense of what has happened to the productivity of schools. Students find meaning in their subcultures. Teachers find meaning in unions and friends. Principals derive meaning from modern management ideologies and promotions. Superintendents dream of finding meaning in a larger district. Parents anchor their meaning in family and work, and on it goes across different groups—individual islands with no common glue to tie them together. The absence of cohesion in many schools is no one's fault. The erosion is the result of two decades of turmoil and foment that has eclipsed the real reasons schools and classrooms exist. The current interest in schools provides an exciting opportunity to rebuild the culture of schools and to reinforce the age-old values and practices that give meaning to the process of education. It is a matter of fusing old with new and celebrating the transformation across a community.

The Core Task of Leadership: Reforming or Recharging?

The external pressures on public schools to change are obvious to anyone. National commissions have pronounced a crisis and suggested several remedies. State governors and legislators seem compelled to demonstrate that they are doing something to improve education—through career ladders, improvement plans, or leadership academics. Less obvious to school principals, district superintendents, and some academics is exactly what these external constituencies want. Legislators seem fairly clear; they want schools restructured. But are these desires echoed at the local level? Do parents and communities want schools to change? Or do interested local groups want schools to change back? Do they want schools reformed, or do they want them renewed? What people want at the local level is less clear. The local ambiguity, coupled with seeming certainty at state and federal levels, creates a fundamental dilemma for educational leadership. If the prevailing ways and practices of schools need changing, then existing cultural patterns make the going extremely rough—as past experience has reaffirmed again and again. If, however, the resilient culture of schools needs reviewing and renewing, then the common interest in education provides an interesting opportunity— if we can only figure out what to do.

Dilemmas, by their nature, are insoluble. The meaning of any enterprise is anchored on symbols, and change produces ambiguity and loss. Worn-out symbols undermine meaning and stimulate hopeful searches for alternatives. Schools now undoubtedly suffer from the residual effects of two decades of innovative improvement and reform. While still reeling from the last efforts to make things different, teachers and principals are again being confronted with demands for more change. They are encouraged to try something new while they still grapple with what they have lost.

Managers solve problems. Leaders confront dilemmas. Leaders reframe impossible dilemmas into novel opportunities. Leaders in organizations across all sectors are confronted with many of the same issues that educators now face: (1) How do we encourage meaning and commitment; (2) how do we deal with loss and change; and (3) how can we shape symbols that convey the essence of the enterprise to insiders and outsiders? Educational leaders must create artful ways to reweave organizational tapestries from old traditions, current realities, and future visions. This work cannot be done by clinging to old ways, emulating principles from effective schools and excellent companies, or divining futuristic images from what we imagine the next decades will be like. Rather, it takes a collective look backward, inward, and ahead—in education on the part of administrators, teachers, parents, students, and other members of a school community. It is a process of transformation akin to the one that produces a butterfly from a caterpillar—a cocoon of human experience in which past, present, and future are fused together in an organic process.

How can a leader move from the metaphoric to a literal course of action? I typically respond to corporate leaders who ask this question, "It will come to you—probably through a time of creative brooding that involves others in the company." This charge produces a bewildered first response, followed in time by some highly creative strategies. Here are some examples from education to create a yeasty foment for reforming while revitalizing the culture of public schools:

1. *Recreate the history of a school.* In New York City, several elementary schools convened groups of parents, teachers, administrators, students, alumni, and retirees in sessions to build the story of a particular school. From the deliberations, people came to see their roots and realities. In all cases, the juxtaposition of past and present created a shared sense of new direction—a shared vision for the school. In the aggregate, these schools showed dramatic improvements in test scores, attendance, vandalism rates, and other measures of school performance.

2. *Articulate shared values.* What a school "stands for" needs to be shared. In top-quality companies, slogans provide a shorthand that makes essential characteristics accessible. Symbols, rituals, and artifacts represent intangible values. One school district, along with a local advertising group, recently made a commercial for its school. The intended audience was twofold (as it is in any advertisement): consumers and workers. The response to the commercials was overwhelmingly positive. Efforts of teachers and students have been reinforced and shared.

3. *Anoint and celebrate heroes.* Every school has a pantheon of heroes—past, present, and future. Their anointment and celebration provides tangible human examples of shared values and beliefs. A recent call to my office from the new principal of my old high school offers a novel example:

"We would like you to visit your alma mater," the principal said.

"Why?" I responded.

"Because you have done all right for yourself," she said, "and from all indicators you weren't supposed to. Your teachers remember you as particularly troublesome. Your classmates recall exploits of mischief rather than demonstrations of academic worth. The records reveal a grade point average that is, at best, unimpressive. The assistant principal notes that you spent more time in her office and the halls than you did in class. Your football coach was certain you'd end up in prison. In short, we want you on campus to show other troublemakers that there may be hope for them."

Countless other similar opportunities to celebrate teachers, students, administrators, or parents who exemplify intangible values exist in every school.

4. *Reinvigorate rituals and ceremonies.* Rituals and ceremonies provide regular and special occasions for learning, celebrating, and binding individuals to traditions and values. The parents of a public high school recently gave a banquet for its teachers. Teachers arrived at the school's cafeteria, greeted by corsages and ribbons labeled with terms such as guru, mentor, or exemplar. The cafeteria tables were draped with white linen tablecloths and

bedecked with silver candelabra with lighted candles. Teachers and parents sang together at a piano, drinking wine and eating cheese. The dinner was potluck; each parent brought a dish. The program, following dinner, called attention to the history, values, and vision of the school. The school choir sang. The event delighted the entire audience—and transformed the school.

The principal of a large high school required his faculty to attend the annual graduation ceremony and wear their academic robes. If requested, the district paid the rental fee. Parents and students received the graduation ceremony with acclaim. The next year, attendance at the event doubled. Drinking and other discipline problems have disappeared. Parent confidence in the school has gone up dramatically.

5. *Tell good stories.* At a recent junior high school faculty meeting, teachers spent the time telling stories about students and each other. As a result, several exemplary students were identified, one a student who had changed from a troublemaker to a top student nearly overnight. In doing so, he overcame nearly insurmountable family and learning problems. The faculty thus convened an awards assembly to recognize all the exemplary students and share their stories with the other students. The most dramatically improved student was awarded a large brass eagle. The award now carries the student's name and is given each year to the one who improves the most.

6. *Work with the informal network of cultural players.* A collection of priests, gossips, and storytellers presides over each school's culture. Often, those roles are occupied by nonprofessionals such as secretaries, food service workers, or custodians. Such people provide important linkages inside and are often a direct conduit to the local community. These people need encouragement. They need recognition. One school named a new patio after a custodian, a man who served an important role as a keeper of the history of the school, conveying to both teachers and students the rich legacy of past exploits and glories. When changes are proposed, the informal network must be intimately involved. Otherwise, these people will sabotage the effort.

Using Outside Pressure to Build from Within

The effective-schools movement and state reform initiatives create external pressures often interpreted as a need to significantly change the culture of public schools. At times, such alternatives may be needed. But rather than following the prescriptions suggested or imposed by others, schools need to look inside themselves, both historically and contemporarily.

Old practices and other losses need to be buried and commemorated. Meaningless practices and symbols need to be analyzed and revitalized. Emerging visions, dreams, and hopes need to be articulated and celebrated. These are the core tasks that will occupy educational leaders for several years to come.

References

Baldridge, J. V. "Organizational Change: Institutional Sagas, External Challenges, and Internal Politics." In *Managing Change in Educational Organizations*, edited by J. V. Baldridge and T. E. Deal. Berkeley: McCutchan, 1975, pp. 427–448.

Baldridge, J. V., and T. E. Deal. "Overview of Change Processes in Educational Organizations." In *Managing Change in Educational Organizations*, edited by J. V. Baldridge and T. E. Deal. Berkeley: McCutchan, 1975, pp. 1–23.

Baldridge, J. V., and T. E. Deal. *The Dynamics of Organizational Change in Education* . Berkeley: McCutchan, 1983.

Bolman, L., and T. E. Deal. *Modern Approaches to Understanding Organizations*. San Francisco: Jossey-Bass, 1984.

Clark, B. "The Organizational Saga in Higher Education." In *Managing Change in Educational Organizations,* edited by J. V. Baldridge and T. E. Deal. Berkeley: McCutchan, 1975, pp. 98–108.

Coleman, J. S. *Equality of Educational Opportunity.* Washington, D.C.: Government Printing Office, 1966.

Corwin, R. G. "Strategies for Organizational Innovation: An Imperical Comparison." *American Sociological Review* 37 (1972): 441–452.

Deal, T. E. "Symbolism of Effective Schools." *Elementary School Journal* 85 (January 1985a): 3.

Deal, T. E. "National Commissions: Blueprints for Remodeling." *Education and Urban Society* 17 (February 1985b): 2.

Deal, T. E., and A. Kennedy. *Corporate Cultures*. Reading, Mass.: Jossey-Bass, 1982.

Halpin, A. W., and D. B. Croft. *The Organizational Climate of Schools*. St. Louis, Mo.: Washington University, 1962.

Marris, P. *Loss and Change*. London: Routledge & Kegan Paul, 1974.

McDill, E., and L. Rigsby. *Structure and Process in Secondary Schools*. Baltimore: John Hopkins University Press, 1973.

McPherson, G. *Small Town Teacher*. Cambridge, Mass.: Harvard University Press, 1972.

Meyer, J., and B. Rowan. "The Structure of Educational Organizations." In *Dynamics of Organizational Change in Education*, edited by J. Baldridge and T. E. Deal. Berkeley: McCutchan, 1983.

Peters, T. J., and R. H. Waterman, Jr. *In Search of Excellence*. New York: Harper & Row, 1982.

Rutter, M., B. Maughan, P. Mortimore, J. Ouston, and A. Smith. *Fifteen Thousand Hours*. Cambridge: Harvard University Press, 1979.

Sarason, S. *The Culture of the School and the Problem of Change*. Boston: Allyn and Bacon, 1971.

Swidler, A. *Organization Without Authority*. Cambridge: Harvard University Press, 1979.

Waller, W. *The Sociology of Teaching*. New York: Wiley, 1932.

2

The Leadership of Educational Clans

Robert G. Owens

A rguably, the organizational context of a high school affects the schooling process because it influences the specific, day-to-day, hour-by-hour experiences of teachers and students. This study explored the connections between organizational variables and the behavior of adults working in the comprehensive senior high school by focusing on the work behavior of the high school principal.

In the mid-1970s, the concept of *loose coupling* enamored students of school organization. By the 1980s, however, it became clear that loose coupling was in itself an inadequate analysis. Weick's (1976) observation that schools are, in part, loosely coupled systems (e.g., core activities such as instruction) and, in part, bureaucratic systems (e.g., supporting activities such as financial and personnel accounting) provides a more comprehensive analysis. But the concept of schools as a dual system is more complicated than the original concept of loose coupling. This dual system begins to hint at the enormous complexity of the schools. Indeed, it now appears that schools are characterized by such organizational complexity that reducing descriptions of them to parsimonious models may remain problematic for some time.

But a tendency to think of all kinds of schools in generic terms further complicates the understanding of their organizational structure. In discussing loose coupling, Weick (1982), for example, spoke of schools without differentiating between elementary schools and senior high schools. Yet, as Firestone and Herriott (1982) pointed out, these two phenotypes differ significantly in organization. Part of the uncertainty in understanding the organizational characteristics of schools comes from the assumption that "a school is a school," not an organization of multiple types.

This study of the work behavior of a senior high school principal was ethnographic. The investigator went into the school and "lived with" the principal full-time for the first half of the school year. During this semester, observations were recorded, people interviewed, and documents from exist-ing files studied. During the second half of the year, the investigator visited the school less frequently, averaging one day a week. The analysis of the data began at this time, using what ethnographers call *theme analysis* (Owens 1982). The major themes that emerged from this study of West Durham Senior High School related to the culture of the organization.

The Culture of West Durham Senior High School

At West Durham Senior High School, the culture overwhelming influ-ences its organizational structure, coordinated cooperative effort, and organi-zational control and discipline. The term *culture* refers to the body of solutions to external and internal problems that has worked consistently for the people in the school and that is therefore taught to new members as the correct way to perceive, think about, and feel in relation to those problems (Schein 1985). Thus, those in the school acquire a "learned pattern of uncon-scious (or semi-conscious) thought, reflected and reinforced by behavior, that silently and powerfully shapes the experience of a people" (Deal 1985). This thought pattern results in agreement, implicit or explicit, among teachers, administrators, and other participants on "the way things are done around here" (Kilmann et al. 1985).

The principal of the school and, indeed, everyone else in the school frequently use the semantics of bureaucracy to express the logic and ra-tionality of their actions. They talk about rules, hierarchical power, chain of command, and the other conventional attributes of bureacracy. But the power of such cultural symbols as organizational history, legends, myths, heroes, stories, rituals, and ceremonies to establish and reinforce shared understand-ings, values, and norms is striking in this school.

A Hero and a Legend

The retelling of stories and legends, the extolling of heroes, and the reinforcing highly valued norms often reiterates and reinforces these cultural norms. Many of these stories and legends, for example, keep alive the memory of Oscar Swenson, who became the first superintendent of schools when the West Durham School District was formed in 1942 and who was still in office at the time of his death in 1972. Although four others have served as superintendent since Swenson, the "Swenson stories" (as they are commonly called by present-day staff members) are told and retold with relish.

As superintendent of schools during the district's years of growth and expansion, Swenson built all of the six schools now in the district. He hired about 80 percent of those now teaching at the high school. Since he consid-ered staffing the schools a high priority, Swenson used to roam the country from Maine to Texas seeking out superior teachers to attract to the district. Thus, although they came from diverse backgrounds, these teachers (as well as the principal and the three assistant principals) were each sought out and recruited by Swenson. Moreover, Swenson nurtured a benevolent pater- nalistic relationship with "his" teachers. He was sensitive to their problems; he cared about the development of their careers; and he demanded loyalty and high professional standard. Staff members readily identify themselves as "Swenson recruits," and they frequently illustrate present-day situations with stories that begin, "Well, you know what Oscar Swenson used to say about that."

A Ritual With Coffee and Cookies

Teachers frequently tell Swenson stories at the weekly ritual known as "coffee and cookies during third and fourth period" in West Durham Senior High School. The chair of the home economics department initiates the ritual by placing a small slip of paper in each staff member's mailbox announcing the day of the eagerly anticipated event. On the appointed day, during the third and fourth periods (between 9:14 and 10:44 in the morning), cookies baked by students in the home economics classes are laid out in the badly worn and threadbare "living room" of the home economics suite, and stu- dents from home economics classes serve coffee. Virtually every faculty member has one of these periods free, and those who do happily converge for the event. Bearing a paper plate of cookies and a cup of coffee, staff members mingle, some standing and circulating, others sitting together in groups, sipping coffee and talking. The school principal, John Dunphy, and his three assistant principals (William Kane, Peter Russo, and Alfredo Bus- cemi) rarely miss these weekly gatherings. They are available to hear news of recent events, to convey the views of the school board and the superintendent of schools on contemporary issues, and to share current problems and issues at the school.

This ritual appears to be at least the rough counterpart of the Friday afternoon "beer bust" so commonly reported in the literature by observers of Hewlett Packard and other electronics firms. Here, teachers check informally with one another and with the administration on what is happening, what they are expected to do, what is valued, and what is unimportant. These informal gatherings, reminiscent of family get-togethers allow teachers who rarely meet one another during passing in the course of the day to maintain contact. The coffee-and-cookies sessions are vital in socializing new faculty members to the values of the school and in nurturing and reinforcing these values for the old-timers. Frequently at these sessions, some of the old- timers—such as John Dunphy, the principal, and Joseph DeMarco, the re- spected chair of the foreign language department—regale the group with "Oscar Swenson stories" that they consider applicable to current problems and dilemmas in the school. Other teachers with a part in the stories and legends being retold supply details; they support the process by providing their own recollections and expressions of commitment to the values the legends portray. Thus, this ritual, repeated from week to week throughout the year, is one way the values of the organization are made clear, are continually reinforced, and are accepted by members of the faculty as their own.

A Highly Socialized Staff

Understanding this merging of personal commitment with organizational values in West Durham High School is not difficult. Teachers and administrators enter school as pupils at the age of five or six. These educators report that they had liked school and had succeeded. With few exceptions, such as a brief time out for military service or child rearing, they have remained in school ever since. In many cases, these educators have virtually continuous participation in schools for periods of 25 to 35 years or more. In fact, partly because of the district's compensation plan, many teachers take graduate courses at nearby universities, thus continuing their roles as students as well as teachers.

West Durham Senior High Schol is an organization whose legitimacy and authority is largely unquestioned by teachers almost completely socialized to its values and goals. The teachers anticipate a lifelong career at the schools. Despite "family-style" bickering and competition among members, alienation is almost nonexistent, coordinated effort is high, and commitment is maximized. The principal secures the teachers' cooperation with minimal use of explicit hierarchical control. This is not an organization that is loosely coupled. It is one that uses clanlike structures as mechanisms of coordination and control. These structures strongly emphasize cultural norms and values, not bureaucratic mechanisms.

Culture as a Bearer of Authority

As Weick's (1976) analysis suggests, the bureaucratic glue in West Durham Senior High School is indeed weak. But the organizational culture provides more than an extremely strong, elastic glue that ensures great cohesiveness in the high school. The school's culture establishes the standards of work behavior. Thus, while hierarchical surveillance of much of the teachers' work is indeed minimal, they receive constant, powerful cues from colleagues on what is acceptable and what is unacceptable on the job. For example, teachers frequently collaborate in developing instructional units or daily lesson plans and in preparing and grading the departmental examinations given in multi-section courses.

Establishing Norms and Values Through Socialization

Two experienced teachers informally instructing a first-year colleague on how to handle the principal's first observation of her teaching also illustrates the power of cultural norms. The beginning teacher, Mrs. Gennaro, was in the teachers' lounge. When two experienced colleagues came into the room, she expressed apprehension to them about the principal's official visit to evaluate her work. One of the experienced teachers, Mr. Costello, said, "Mr. Dunphy will want a seat in the back row, the last seat on the left as you face the class. He'll want to sit there. If you have a student in that seat, move him out now. Then there won't be any problem when Mr. Dunphy comes into the room." Mrs. Gennaro thanked him for the suggestion and told him she would act on it. Mr. Costello continued, "Be sure to have a structured lesson. Structured dialogue would be good, something in which the kids have a chance to talk and show that they are learning something."

The second experienced teacher, Mrs. Johnson, had been leaning toward Mrs. Gennaro, nodding supportively. "Yes," she joined in, "have a structured lesson, and be sure you have introduced the unit beforehand. Don't try to introduce a new unit when you are having an observation." "Oh, no!" Mr. Costello agreed. "Don't try to start a new unit while he's there. Introduce the unit the day before. Then, when he's there, you can say, 'Now as we learned earlier, blah, blah, blah.' So you can show what you're doing builds on what has gone before."

"And," added Mrs. Johnson, "be sure that whatever the lesson is, it is something that all the kids can get in on. Don't leave anyone out. Be sure that everyone speaks and gets involved in the lesson." "Oh, yeah," Mr. Costello agreed, "that's right. You have to show that the lesson is suitable for everyone in the class. It's a good idea to call on people who aren't talking. Cover the whole class, people in the corners of the room, then go to the middle. Don't let only a few people do the talking." As the conversation developed, the two experienced teachers supportively drew closer to their younger colleague, going into further detail on how to orchestrate the lesson that Mr. Dunphy was going to observe and evaluate.

A Multicultural Organization

One of the dominant characteristics of the culture of West Durham High School is the high value placed on the authority of the institution. The administrators' behavior consistently reveals this value. The principal and his three assistants spend much of their time emphasizing to teachers the need to exercise institutional control over students. The elaborate and carefully supervised duty rosters assigning teachers to patrol the corridors and grounds throughout the day, the active and heavily staffed office for attendance and discipline, and the elaborate in-school suspension program all stress the importance of institutional control.

The eight-person guidance department, on the other hand, strongly believes students should be free to exercise informed self-control. This opposing view leads to conflict, sometimes heated, when administrators ask guidance counselors to put pressure on students to enroll in undersubscribed elective courses. The counselors, of course, maintain that they are not administrators. To coerce their students would violate ethical values and would undermine what they consider important educational goals of the school.

Similarly, the teachers in the special education unit see their roles in a remarkably different way from the other teachers in the school. They tend, for example, to act as ombudsmen for their charges. They intercede for students wherever they see potential problems, enlisting the special aid of other staff members to meet the needs of students with handicapping conditions. They consult with other teachers to solve classroom problems involving special education students. As the chair of the guidance department observed, "They don't let their kids fail; they don't let them fall through the cracks; they make sure that this school works' for their kids. How different it is with the kids in 'regular classes' who cut classes and miss out on assignments they couldn't do in the first place. When they fall behind in their work, the teacher says, OK, you make up all that you missed, and we'll let you come back to class. Well, they couldn't do the work in the first place, and now they have a double load to do. They're doomed to failure. They fall through the cracks." "Regular" teachers, in other words, play a more limited role in dealing with students. They often take the attitude that students not "making it" should be removed from the class and sent elsewhere.

Thus, while the school as a whole exhibits a recognizable, describable organizational culture that powerfully shapes the perceptions and behavior of staff members, subcultures clearly exist within the school. Norms and values and, indeed, heroes and stories vary from department to department. Teachers easily recognize these subcultures. For example, they often exchange comments (sometimes lightheartedly, occasionally in anger) over well-understood conflicting values and norms between those in academic departments and those in physical education.

West Durham Senior High School as a Clan

The metaphor of the clan (Ouchi and Price 1978; Ouchi 1981) aply describes this school:

1. There is high agreement among members as to what constitutes proper behavior.

2. There is high agreement among members regarding what is legitimate authority, and this agreement is rooted in the traditions of the group rather than some rational formulation.

3. The beliefs and values of the organization are communicated through a system of rituals and ceremonies (rather than codified in law and detailed rules).

4. Staffing patterns are relatively stable, with expectations for long-term, if not lifetime, employment.

5. Recruitment is selective, followed by intensive socialization; together, these result in high levels of loyalty and commitment to the values and traditions of the clan.

Predictably, this clan-like organization has developed a strong culture that is extremely powerful in controlling the behavior of participants and is the dominant influence in evoking the cooperative effort normally associated with organization. Three themes emerge from the observations in this study: This clan is impoverished, embattled, and professional.

An Impoverished Clan

At the time of the study, this clan had been down-at-the-heels for over a decade. Money comes hard here. Tax levy proposals for the annual school district budget had been routinely defeated at the polls in nine of the ten years preceding the study, resulting in budgets gutted of all but the bare essentials.

For example, although enrollments had been falling dramatically for years, there were not enough student desks to go around. The furniture (most of it then over 25 years old) was breaking down, and no one remembered replacement purchases. Similarly, students in the office practice and business education rooms take turns pounding on worn-out typewriters because so many machines are broken. For years, there has been neither a service contract nor replacement of the equipment, and the skimpy funds budgeted for repairs no longer come near to keeping the equipment going. When asked what plans the business education department had for getting into word processing and electronic technology, the chair scoffed, "Are you kidding? Even if we could get the money to buy the equipment, how would we maintain it? Who would replace the software as it wears out under the heavy use in a place like this? I can cannibalize some of our old manual typewriters to keep a few of our machines going, but you can't do that with computers. I'm trained in word processing. We've got teachers here who have been studying computers and are really into all of that. But where do we get the money to support a program?"

The school has student lockers in the corridors. Each locker is equipped with a lock, for which students are issued keys. Over the years, locks broke and keys were lost, and budget requests for repairs were "deferred." At the same time, allocations for clerical personnel were reduced, so office staff no longer supervised locker maintenance. As a result, the day came when there were not enough functioning lockers to assign one to each student, even though enrollments were down. Parents protested to the Board of Education; to get around the problem, the school now assigns a classroom teacher for two periods each day to take charge and straighten out the matter. The costs of his services are concealed under the instruction category of the budget, rather than appearing as a maintenance cost.

When the Board of Education directed that one copy of each textbook be sent to the board room to form a library of textbooks that would be open to the public, the teachers were dismayed. Did the Board of Education not know that the battered textbooks that they did have were still insufficient to go around? Indeed, they were using ingenious schemes for students to share those that were available.

An Embattled Clan

For many years, the politics of governing in the school district has been fierce. Nearly continuous bruising battles have long since divided the community into two adversarial camps. The teachers speak matter-of-factly of the "white hats" (Board of Education members and their constituencies generally seen as supporting the teachers' view of schooling) and the "black hats" (generally seen as arch-conservatives opposed to all but minimal schooling).

These grinding, embittered political battles have had a powerful impact on the clan as the tides of fortune favored first one side in the community and then another, with superintendents of schools coming and going as a result. Staving off reductions in traditional programs and services has long been a central preoccupation of the clan. It has probably resulted in little more than slowing the steady erosion over time. Clan members speak of "being in the trenches," "fighting a rear-guard action," being "under fire," with their proposals to improve the school program getting "blown out of the water." The concept of "surviving" arises frequently in their conversations.

A Professional Clan

The clan members are well-educated, extensively trained professionals whose provenance is wide-ranging. They take great pride in their competence in specialized subprofessions—for example, English teacher, science teacher, school psychologist, counsellor, social worker. They are actively involved in maintaining ties with professional peers outside of the district through attending conferences, participating in associations, and taking graduate courses. An on-site visit to the school by the 30-member Middle States Association evaluation team was an energizing professional "shot in the arm" for the clan. They saw it as legitimating and supporting their values and their claims to professional competence.

The Principal as Clan Leader

Those principals who would be powerful leaders in schools must be prepared to go beyond the merely routine minimums suggested by the time-honored two-dimensional models of leadership derived from the Ohio State studies (Stogdill 1974). They must be prepared to engage in symbolic leadership and to develop organizational cultures of a new and higher order. Such leaders attend to the creation of new legends and fresh organizational stories; they extol emerging heroes and develop new social norms in the organization.

John Dunphy, the principal of West Durham Senior High School, was trying to provide this leadership. For example, staff members know he has a high regard for the Humanities Program. This cross-discipline program uses team teaching and planning, employs a rich variety of pedagogic techniques, and draws on a variety of human and instructional resources. Dunphy frequently expresses support and approval of these practices. He rarely misses an opportunity to talk about the program with other teachers, parent groups, the school district administration, and the Board of Education. Often he spends time in the facilities occupied by the Humanities Program, talking with students, having coffee with the teaching team, and occasionally participating in classes.

He obviously supports, almost defers to, Joseph DeMarco, the chair of the foreign language department and head of the Humanities Program. Dunphy often asks DeMarco to serve on influential committees and regularly seeks his advice on what should be said about school issues in speeches and public statements. DeMarco's status, and his success in working with his faculty team, is plainly visible to other teachers in the school. By the time of the study, Dunphy had begun to express his hope that the Humanities Program would become the core of a major shift in the way that the school organized its instructional program. He was delighted that the chair of the Board of Education had caught on to the idea and strongly supported an expanded Humanities Program as the core of the high school curriculum to be developed for all students in the school. A new hero appeared to be in the making at West Durham Senior High School.

Thus, through symbolic leadership, Dunphy signals and demonstrates to others in the clan what is important, what is valued, what is wanted, what goals override others. He creates and communicates a vision for others in the clan, describing a desired state of affairs, one better than the present. Through symbolic leadership, he creates and communicates a new sense of purpose for subordinates. He helps them to understand that a new tradition is essential to the success of the overall mission and that each member has a role to play in it.

Dunphy does not assume that everyone sees the whole picture. He uses words (oral and written) and other symbols (such as time, attention, and his personal presence) to continually emphasize what is important, what is good, what is wanted. He tries to make clear to subordinates in the clan the connections between what they do *and what they could do* to enhance the realization of the clan's central values.

There is a precondition for symbolic leadership. Leaders must think clearly about what is important. They must develop a vision about a desired state of affairs that is clear to them, one they can articulate to others. Indeed, symbolic leadership is not possible unless the leader has carefully developed a vision of what should be with some substance. The vision must have some quality that can stir the consciousness of others and induce their commitment to sharing it as their own purpose. The symbolic leader, after all, stands for something that is important and that gives meaning and purpose to the seemingly mundane and routine work of others in the school. This *something*, this vision, this desired better state of affairs, must receive careful thought. If ever planning is called for, symbolic leadership calls for it.

But even symbolic leadership is insufficient to provide excellence in schooling. The research of such pioneers as Stern (1970) and Halpin and Croft (1962) stressed that a distinctive organizational climate characterizes excellent schools and seems to set such schools apart from all others. Later studies, including the work of Sarason (1971), have extended this concept, revealing that each school has a particular *culture* that is describable and highly specific. Each school has a uniqueness, a history, traditions and customs, that leaders emphasize and make coherent. The leaders of schools take care not only to preserve the traditions that already exist, but also begin to build new higher-order traditions. Building an organizational culture means building behavior norms that exemplify the best a school stands for. It means building an institution that people believe in strongly, that they identify with personally as an ideological system, and that they render their loyalty to gladly. All this gives meaning to the work people do, thus motivating teachers and other staff members.

To build strong organizational cultures in schools, leaders spend time articulating the purpose and the mission of the school. They socialize others to these values. They define and redefine the uniqueness of the school. They develop and keep before people reinforcing systems of symbols. They reward those who accept and reflect the desired norms and values of the school. If West Durham Senior High School is an indicator, these schools are not primarily bureaucracies. They are not characterized by the impersonality of the system of rules and formal policies. The strong bonding that occurs between people, and between people and organizations, matters. Under cultural leadership, students and teachers both understand they are part of an important and worthwhile larger mission. This feeling, in itself, gives meaning to their daily efforts: They are part of something special and important. Under cultural leadership, therefore, students and teachers find satisfaction in being part of a special group whose excellence is rooted in a tradition of achievement and high standards.

All schools have cultures of one kind or another. The culture of a school is not necessarily and, assuredly, not automatically supportive of education and achievement. Developing the kind of culture that supports high levels of motivation and learning requires skilled, strong, planned leadership. For example, at the time of this study, North Durham High School (about five miles from West Durham Senior High School) developed a culture dominated by divisiveness, resistance to authority, denigration of learning, and control by gangs of students. The school became "turf" to be controlled and defended, and students soon learned to give allegiance to the gangs that ran the place. In time, the teachers and administrators lost control of the school, and only through considerable police involvement did a semblance of order and control return.

The culture of that school, as in every school, shapes and molds how people think, feel, and behave. It is communicated through customs, traditions, expectations, common meanings, norms, and habits. It is visible in words and behavior of all kinds as people go about their daily activities, for it is ordinary daily behavior that reveals values, beliefs, and commitment. The culture of a school is a constructed reality, after all, and it takes strong, skilled, dedicated leadership to construct a vision of reality that coalesces students and teachers alike to moving ahead together toward higher levels of excellence.

Conclusion

Four conclusions emerged from the observation and analysis of West Durham Senior High School:

1. The concept of loosely coupled systems is not useful in analyzing the data from this study. Loose coupling appears meaningful only if the coupling expected is the mechanistic sort normally associated with Weberian classical bureaucracy.

2. Powerful integrating linkages in the senior high school are instrumental in unifying the participants in a coordinated effort to achieve common values. These linkages are the warp and woof of the culture of the organization.

3. The clan is a useful metaphor for describing the structure, the "glue," that coheres the school's members. The nearly total socialization of the clan members is highly motivating; it legitimates the authority system and ensures predictable job performance without close, detailed surveillance by the hierarchy.

4. Leaders of educational clans must devote time and skill to both symbolic leadership and culture development if they seek to lift the organization from functional adequacy toward educational excellence.

The notion of the clan as an organizational structure is supported in the literature. In 1945, Mayo pondered his research in the light of the awful disaster of World War II. In *The Social Problems of Industrial Civilization*, he noted that a major shift in social organization had taken place during the Industrial Revolution. The old order, which promoted and regulated cooperative human endeavor through the clan structure in society, had given way to a new, depersonalized type of formal organization. Mayo recognized World War II as only one disaster that would befall mankind if newer ways of organizing cooperative human effort, more in harmony with the values and techniques of the age-old clan structure, were not found and used in the industrial and post-industrial eras. "Such societies," he said of clans, "know no loyalty outside of their own group. The desire of every individual member to cooperate in communal activities is spontaneous and complete." This loyalty is the essence of the clan.

Ten years later, Selznick (1957), struggling to illuminate the problem of administrators exercising leadership, used the term *institutionalization* to describe a strikingly similar notion:

Institutionalization refers to those processes and methods by which the organization inculcates a set of strategic values in the individuals who work in the organization. Institutionalization means to infuse with value beyond the technical requirements of the task at hand. . . . From the standpoint of the committed person, the organization is changed from an expendable tool to a valued source of personal satisfaction. Therefore the art of the creative leader is the art of institutional-building . . . to fashion an organism that embodies new and enduring values.

Thus, value rationality, not goal rationality, dominates Selznick's description of the organization. In contrast to Weber (1947), Selznick emphasized the organization as an ideological and normative habitat for the individual.

Building on these ideas more recently, Meyer and Rowan (1983) pointed out that the institutionalization of myths has become an important source of formal structure. For example, ". . . rationalized professions emerge, and these . . . are controlled, not only by direct inspection of work outcomes, but also by social rules of licensing, certifying, and schooling . . . the delegation of activities to the appropriate occupations is socially accepted and often legally obligatory. . . ." Therefore, these "institutionalized myths" largely define the school's structure. While *teacher* is a generalized professional category, it encompasses such specialized categories as counselor, librarian, special education teacher, art teacher, social worker, school psychologist, and nurse-teacher.

The individuals in these numerous categories experience a high sense of what Durkheim (1933, 1961) called *solidarity*. They are necessarily dependent on one another to achieve their collectively held professional goals. Often stated as values, these goals are ambiguous. Determining how individual performance affects outcomes is difficult; and the high inclusion and virtually complete socialization of the professional participants characterizes the organization. Indeed, this high degree of socialization, this virtually complete merging of the teachers' individual goals with the espoused values of the organization, is the outstanding characteristic of the high school.

Obviously, symbolic clan leadership goes beyond the essentials of managing a good school. Perhaps not so apparently, symbolic leadership does not "just happen." The clan's values must be pondered, new goals envisioned, and plans for achieving them laid.

The clan leader must, for example, signal to others what is important and what is valuable. Such a leader tours the school, visits classrooms, seeks out students, and spends time with them. She seeks out opportunities to preside at ceremonies and rituals symbolizing and supporting the goals and values she intends to emphasize. The symbolic clan leader tends to minimize engaging in management activities in favor of underscoring the activities important to maintaining and developing the central values that define the culture of the clan.

In many senior high schools, the central values may well be expressed in sports, the marching band, and other extracurricular activities. The cultural values of other schools may be better expressed in educational and creative achievement. The symbolic educational leader must be a friendly critic of the culture of the high school—one who creates a new vision of an educationally better culture in the school and then plans to organize his time and energies to communicate that vision to students and teachers alike. A vision provides the clear sense of order and direction needed to form a consensus on what school is really all about—a consensus all can commit themselves to whole-heartedly.

References

Deal, T. E. "Cultural Change: Opportunity, Silent Killer or Metamorphosis?" In *Gaining Control of the Corporate Culture*, edited by R. H. Kilmann, M. J. Saxton, and R. Serpa. San Francisco: Jossey-Bass, 1985.

Durkheim, E. *The Division of Labor in Society*. Translated by G. Simpson. New York: The Free Press, 1933.

Durkheim, E. *The Elementary Forms of the Religious Life*. New York: Collier Books.

Firestone, W., and R. Herriott. "Prescriptions for Effective Elementary Schools Don't Fit Secondary Schools." *Educational Leadership* 40 (December 1982): 51–53.

Halpin, A. W., and D. B. Croft. *The Organizational Climate of Schools*. USOE Research Project, Contract no. SAE 543–8639, 1962.

Kilmann, R. H., M. J. Saxton, and R. Serpa. "Five Key Issues in Understanding and Changing Culture." In *Gaining Control of the Corporate Culture*, edited by R. H. Kilmann, M. J. Saxton, and R. Serpa. San Francisco: Jossey-Bass, 1985.

Mayo, E. *The Social Problems of an Industrial Civilization*. Boston: Division of Research, Graduate School of Business Administration, Harvard University, 1945.

Meyer, J. W., and B. Rowan. "Institutionalized Organizations: Formal Structure as Myth and Ceremony." In *Organizational Environments: Ritual and Rationality*, edited by J. W. Meyer and R. S. Scott. Beverly Hills: Sage Publications, 1983.

Ouchi, W. G., and R. W. Price. "Hierarchies, Clans and Theory Z. A New Perspective on Organization Development." *Organizational Dynamics* 24(Autumn 1978): 44.

Ouchi, W. G. *Theory Z*. Reading, Mass: Addison-Wesley, 1981.

Owens, R. G. "Methodological Rigor in Naturalistic Inquiry: Some Issues and Answers." *Educational Administration*, 18(1982): 1–21.

Sarason, S. B. *The Culture of the School and the Problem of Change.* San Francisco: Jossey-Bass, 1971.

Schein, E. H. "How Culture Forms, Develops and Changes." In *Gaining Control of the Corporate Culture,* edited by R. H. Kilmann, J. J. Saxton, and R. Serpa. San Francisco, Jossey-Bass, 1985.

Selznick, P. *Leadership in Administration.* New York: Harper and Row, 1985.

Stern, G. G. *People in Context: Measuring Person-Environment Congruence in Education and Industry.* New York: John Wiley and Sons, 1970.

Stogdill, R. M. *Handbook of Leadership: A Survey of Theory and Research.* New York: The Free Press, 1974.

Weber, M. 1947. *The Theory of Social and Economic Organization.* Translated by A. Henderson and T. Parsons. New York: Macmillan, 1947.

Weick, K. E. "Administering Education in Loosely Coupled Schools." *Phi Delta Kappan,* 63(1982): 673–676.

Weick, K. E. "Educational Organizations as Loosely Coupled Systems" *Administrative Science Quarterly* 21 (1976).

3

The School Principal: Scapegoat or the Last Great Hope?

David C. Dwyer, Bruce G. Barnett, Ginny V. Lee

I n recent years, our nation's schools have suffered a serious loss of public confidence. The public's support dwindled as a steady stream of stories emerged about violence in the schools, declining student achievement, and the poor preparation and performance of teachers. A panel of educational leaders delivered the final blow when it concluded that our schools had deteriorated to such an extent that "our nation is at risk" (National Commission on Excellence in Education 1983).

Into this troubled arena—into its very center—the school principal has been thrust by those who have studied "effective" schools, for these researchers have successfully resurrected an old maxim: effective principal, effective school (e.g., Armor et al. 1976, Brookover et al. 1973, Venezky and Winfield 1979, Weber 1971, Wynne 1981). Edmonds (1979, 32) for example, asserted,

One of the most tangible and indispensable characteristics of effective schools is strong administrative leadership, without which the disparate elements of good schooling can neither be brought together nor kept together.

The public embraced this image of strong leadership, partly because it was eager for a solution to schooling's apparent plight, partly because of its persistent belief that great men and women do make history. Thus, school

This chapter was supported by a contract from the National Institute of Education, Department of Education, under Contract No. 400-83-0003. The contents do not necessarily reflect the views or policies of the Department of Education or the National Institute of Education.

principals found themselves in the spotlight, expected to shoulder the awesome responsibility of school reform.

Ironically, as the effective-school researchers forcibly argued their position, other researchers built a convincing case that principals were *not* potent instructional leaders in schools. Goldhammer (1971) found that principals themselves complained that their power and autonomy as school leaders had decreased and that they made fewer decisions regarding instruction at the school level. Other researchers looked for evidence of leadership in the activities of principals but reported, somewhat disparagingly, that they found little in the frenetic, mostly verbal interactions characterizing the principal's day (Morris et al. 1984). Another study (Martin and Willower 1981) likened the principal's work to private-sector management. This study, too, concluded that principals' work is characterized by "variety, brevity, and fragmentation" (p. 79) and that most of the principals' activities (84.8 percent) involve "purely verbal elements" (p. 80).

These researchers concluded that the principal's role as an instructional leader is relatively minor. Morris and his associates (1971) stated "Instructional leadership (in terms of classroom observation and teacher supervision) is *not* the central focus of the principalship" (p. 689). But Martin and Willower (1981, 83) reported:

Perhaps the most widely heralded role of the principal is that of instructional leader, which conjures up images of a task routine dominated by the generation of innovative curricula and novel teaching strategies. The principals in this study spent 17.4 percent of their time on instructional matters . . . the majority of the routine education of youngsters that occurred in the schools was clearly the province of the teaching staff.

Another recent study by Newsburg and Glatthorn (1983) also concluded, "For the most part principals do not provide instructional leadership."

While this debate over the principal's role and potency as an instructional leader continues at the theoretical level, principals are being held accountable for students' academic performance and achievement scores. In some instances, parent groups have demanded the removal of principals who lead schools where children perform below expectations on standardized achievement tests. Are principals simply convenient scapegoats for the woes of education, or are they the last great hope—the source of leadership that will restore the nation's confidence in the public schools?

Finding Meaning in an "Undifferentiated Jumble"

The inability of these studies to resolve the debate over the role of the principal lies in their overly narrow concept of instructional leadership. The studies depended on a perspective that is implicitly rational and bureaucratic, although principals work in organizations better construed as "loosely coupled" (Meyer and Rowan 1978; Weick 1976) or even "disorderly" (Perrow

1982). The inevitable consequence of this narrow perspective is to restrict investigators' concerns to only those behaviors directly and formally tied to instruction, a tiny percentage of principals' activities that researchers actually witness. Yet many researchers abandon any attempt to examine the antecedents and consequences of the vast majority of principals' actions. Morris and others (1984) wrote, for example, "Everything seems to blend together in an undifferentiated jumble of activities that are presumably related, however remotely, to the ongoing rhythm and purpose of the larger enterprise" (p. 689).

Our work, however, has led us to believe that principals can be key agents in the creation of successful school settings and that their potency lies within that previously "undifferentiated jumble" of principal behaviors. Instructional leadership in schools accrues from the repetition of routine acts performed in accord with principals' overarching perspectives of schooling.

Our understanding of the importance of principals' routine activities emerged from the nearly 2,000 hours we spent in 17 schools over a 2-year period. During that time, we "shadowed" and interviewed 17 men and women who led diverse urban, suburban, and rural schools, probing their strategies and observing the consequences of their activities. Each of these principals had been nominated as a successful instructional leader by their superiors. We also observed and interviewed teachers and students, discovering their perspectives on the meaning of the work of these principals.

When we analyzed the nearly 10,000 pages of descriptive material yielded by this field study intended to discover simply what principals do, we found that nine categories of routine behavior summarized their activities: (1) goal setting and planning; (2) monitoring; (3) evaluating; (4) exchanging information; (5) scheduling, allocating resources, and organizing; (6) staffing; (7) modeling; (8) governing; and (9) filling in. We found that more than 50 percent of our observations fit the exchanging-information category and that monitoring, scheduling/allocating resources/organizing, and governing encompassed most of the remaining observations. An analysis of our interviews with teachers about what principals do produced a nearly identical profile. This list of categories is similar to other investigators' inventories (e.g., Martin and Willower 1981) and confirms what others have indicated: Principals' work is largely characterized by face-to-face, verbal transactions, and by fragmentation and brevity.

The duration and intensity of the study allowed us to probe principals' intents and to observe the consequences of many of their actions. These purposes—the targets of their activities—were not always transparent. Consequences sometimes lagged a good deal behind a principal's action. In some instances, only lengthy interviews with various school participants revealed the consequences of principals' actions. The analysis of our observations and interviews produced another list of categories comprising the apparent intents of the principals' efforts in their schools: (1) the distal and proximal elements of schools' work structures associated with the delivery of instruction; (2) staff relations; (3) student relations; (4) safety and order; (5) plant and equipment; (6) community relations; (7) relationships with the district and other institutions; and (8) the school's ethos—its overall tone, spirit, or organizational identity.

Combining the nine types of routine behavior previously discussed with these eight targets or purposes provides a matrix of 72 discrete *action* cells. This formulation or display reveals patterns in the previously chaotic impressions of principals' actions. In our study, the patterns of only eight or nine actions usually accounted for up to 95 percent of the activities we observed. Exchanging information about work structure, monitoring student or staff relations, or governing safety and order in the school, for example, were common principal actions. Sometimes, specific patterns of principals' actions were related to contextual or personal idiosyncrasies in the settings; sometimes, they could be attributed to principals' carefully reasoned approaches. But in all instances, interesting leadership stories emerged; principals strived within their limits to set conditions for, or the parameters of, instruction.

These routine actions, then, seem to be the common acts that principals use to assess the working status of their organizations and the progress of their schools. They are the acts that allow principals to alter the course of events midstream: to return aberrant student behavior to acceptable norms; to suggest changes in teaching style or to demonstrate a preferred form of instruction; to encourage student, teacher, or community support for programs already under way; to develop an awareness of changes needed in the organization.

The success of these actions for instructional management and leadership hinges on principals' capacities to connect them to their own overarching perspectives of the purposes of schooling and of the instructional systems of their schools. The principals we worked with tacitly held such overarching perspectives; most could articulate these perspectives when asked. Their perspectives were complex constellations of personal experiences and beliefs, community and district "givens," principals' behavior, and instructional climate and organizational variables that offered both direct and circuitous routes for the principals to use to influence their schools and the experiences their students encountered daily (fig. 3.1).

The following description of the work of Frances Hedges, principal of Orchard Park Elementary School, reveals one such constellation.[1] Through her ordinary but rigorously applied routine behaviors, Hedges realized her

---

[1]Pseudonyms are used throughout to protect the anonymity of the participants of our study.

Fig. 3.1 The Principal's Role in Instructional Management

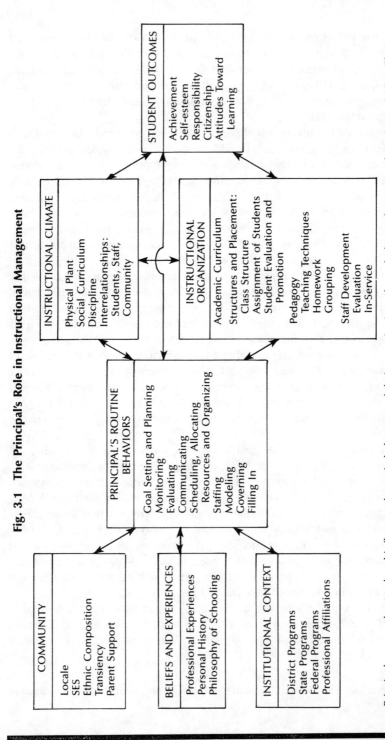

Principals can understand and influence the varied elements of their organizations through the performance of routine activities. Their success hinges on their ability to connect their actions to an overarching perspective of their school settings and their aspirations for students.

vision of schooling. This is a story of an exemplary instructional leader in action.

A Case in Point

The Setting and the Actors

The year 1982 marked Orchard Park Elementary School's 35th year in the city of Hillsdale. Surrounding the school were rows of white, gray, pale green, and pastel yellow houses with neatly trimmed yards. The neighborhood was quiet, but the noise from a nearby freeway attested to its urban setting. The community's only distinctive landmark was an old church that occupied a large corner lot adjacent to the school. The church's three onion-shaped spires had for years cast a sense of permanence over the entire community.

"Permanent," however, would be a somewhat misleading description of the area. Before 1960, white, middle-class families of Italian descent predominated the neighborhood. Over the next few years, increasing numbers of ethnic minorities moved out of the city's poorer neighborhoods to areas like Orchard Park's community, seeking better schools and better living conditions. As a result, Orchard Park's neighborhood lost its homogeneity, and some of its quiet, as several racial conflicts marred the community's tranquility. The school was also affected; educators had to adapt to the needs of the new students. According to Frances Hedges, Orchard Park's principal, the change in the community's composition increased the percentage of students performing below the 50th percentile on the school's standardized achievement tests.

During the year of our study, Orchard Park Elementary School comprised a diversity of racial and ethnic groups. District records showed that as many as ten different language groups were represented in the school's student population. Most of the students were black (59 percent); 13 percent were of Spanish heritage; 16 percent were Asian (Chinese, Filipino, Samoan, Laotian, and Vietnamese); and 11 percent were white. Other ethnic groups composed the remaining 1 percent.

The families of these students were of low-income, or lower-middle-income status. Most parents worked as unskilled laborers (58 percent); 26 percent held skilled or semiskilled jobs; 6 percent were semiprofessionals; only 2 percent were described as professionals. The principal reported that Orchard Park's parents were a supportive group that trusted her judgment in most matters. Because both parents in most households worked, however, active participation on school committees and in classrooms was restricted to a small core group.

Orchard Park employed 25 teachers. Seven of these teachers had more than ten years of experience, and four had been employed as teachers for seven to ten years. Another five had four to six years of experience, and nine had worked in schools for one to three years. Although their instructional approaches differed markedly, there were few signs of negativism, criticism, or conflict among these teachers. Generally, they were supportive of the school and particularly of the principal. One teacher told us that there was only one reason for staff turnover at Orchard Park—retirement. At the end of the year of our study, the staff, together with the community, rallied to prevent the transfer of their principal and came together to hold a "principal appreciation" gathering to honor Hedges's leadership.

The center of attention at that ceremony, Frances Hedges, was a 60-year-old black woman who had served at Orchard Park for six and a half years. She conveyed to all who met her a sense of elegance through her well-matched clothes, golden earrings, oversized glasses, and neatly fashioned white hair. Her appearance contrasted with the casual style most of her staff adopted; she was easily distinguished as the person in charge.

Long before coming to Orchard Park, Hedges had attended a teachers' college in her hometown, originally intending to become a child psychologist. But economic considerations prevented her from pursuing this goal. Instead, she spent 21 years as a classroom teacher, mostly in the district that includes Orchard Park. After receiving a master's degree in educational administration, she gradually climbed to her current position by working as a reading resource teacher, a district program coordinator, and a vice principal.

Hedges's manner with staff and students was personable. Whether discussing professional matters or making small talk, she conveyed warmth and friendliness. She generously complimented the students and teachers. She also communicated often and comfortably through touches, hugs, and embraces. Both students and teachers frequently referred to her as Orchard Park's "mother figure."

Hedges's manner was consistent with her philosophy. She strongly adhered to what she termed "humanistic" beliefs about education: "My philosophy is that if we are warm and humane and nurturing, we maximize the learning of children. There is just no way to separate out those basic needs." Believing she was "acutely sensitive to . . . children's needs as well as adults' needs," Hedges worked to keep everyone "reasonably happy" and to help everyone strengthen their self-esteem.

Attending to the basic needs of children logically led to Hedges's attention to safety and order in her school. She was a strict disciplinarian and never hesitated to reprimand children for misbehavior. But she always tried to help the children understand their mistakes and become more responsible for their own behavior. "I believe that if we are really going to change the behavior of children, we can't just say, 'stop that,' without going a step further and really having some kind of dialogue about what took place, why, and what are the options," she said.

Her philosophy of education also included tenets about instruction. She strongly believed in the importance of academics, particulary reading: "Reading is by far our number-one priority. I believe that if children don't know how to read, they really cannot make it in this world." Thus, Hedges's beliefs about education were related to her concerns for both the social and academic well-being of her students. Her goals for the school reflected these convictions.

Hedges's primary goal at Orchard Park was to build a program conducive to the emotional and social growth of her students. She wanted her staff to instill in each child a love for learning and to foster an awareness of social responsibility. She insisted that her staff actively try to strengthen the children's self-esteem. These goals, she believed, were an essential foundation for building successful academic experiences.

The principal always stated her concern for the students' academic growth from a "whole-child" perspective: "We work very hard to try to make sure that in the six or seven years that boys and girls are in elementary school, that they leave this school operating at grade level or above. . . . I'd like to see them at grade level for at least their last two years so that they can go into junior high school as much stronger and more confident children."

Hedges actively promoted her social and academic goals to the faculty. During the year of our study, she used a district mandate to develop and implement an integrated, three-year instructional plan as a major vehicle for communicating her goals and developing her staff's commitment to them. When we interviewed the teachers about their beliefs and goals, we found that, in virtually all instances, their statements echoed Hedges's own.

Hedges's Enactment of Instructional Leadership

After completing our field study at Orchard Park, we sorted the hundreds of activities we had observed and discussed with participants into the action matrix composed of the principal's routine behavior and purposes described earlier. (See Dwyer et al. [1984] for the full report and analysis of Hedges's leadership.) We found that 80 percent of Hedges's routine actions fell within only 10 of the 72 possible action cells. Rank ordered, her most routine activities included:

> Information exchange/Work structure (16 percent)
> Information exchange/Student relations (10 percent)
> Scheduling, allocating resources/Work structure (9 percent)
> Monitoring/Work structure (9 percent)
> Governing/Safety and order (9 percent)
> Information Exchange/Staff relations (7 percent)
> Monitoring/Safety and order (5 percent)
> Planning and goal setting/Work structure (5 percent)
> Information exchange/Institutional ethos (5 percent)
> Information exchange/Safety and order (5 percent).

Like every other principal participating in the study, Hedges favored direct, face-to-face interaction with students and teachers. In total, 51.5 percent of her activities were verbal exchanges of varying length. Hedges's "jumble" of activities was mostly intended to affect targets directly or indirectly related to instruction. Particularly when we considered the givens in the Orchard Park system and Hedges's personal experiences and beliefs, the way she used these routine actions as occasions to make suggestions, to initiate changes and development, and to encourage teachers to improve their instruction became apparent. Hedges directed these routine effects along two related avenues: instructional climate and instructional organization.

Establishing the Instructional Climate. We treat school climate (a notion embraced by all the principals we worked with) as an observable and changeable characteristic of schools. For our principals, climate encompassed both physical and social aspects of the school environment. Changing a school's climate could entail anything from painting walls to organizing how students lined up at recess. One principal commented, "School climate starts at the curb." In general, our principals perceived climate as a diverse set of properties that would communicate to students that schools are pleasant but serious workplaces designed to help them achieve.

Hedges, too, believed in the importance this concept. Many of her routine actions had direct consequences on the climate at Orchard Park. Both the value she placed on students' emotional well-being and her goal to improve students' self-esteem contributed to a vision of school climate as an important end in itself. In addition, her beliefs about schools and schooling linked climate to instruction: She considered students' emotional well-being an important precursor to learning; she regarded an orderly, disciplined environment as a necessary condition for teaching and learning to take place; and she believed that the improvement of teachers' instructional practices was best achieved in a setting that built on the positive aspects of their skills. Thus, she worked to maintain an environment that contributed to the happiness, safety, and productivity of the students and teachers.

As Hedges supervised students in the building and on the playgrounds, she maintained safety and order at the school and built students' self-esteem. She monitored their conduct and corrected them when necessary, exchanging her views about responsible behavior and reinforcing school rules. She constantly reminded students to pick up trash, bus their trays in the cafeteria, play in the correct areas of the playgrounds, walk instead of run in the hallways, and refrain from pushing and shoving. She used these same actions to carry out her more social goals; she frequently stopped to talk to students, expressing delight at seeing them or remarking about the clothes they were wearing. Children often approached her to describe important events in their lives. Many of these brief interactions concluded with a hug between the principal and the child. These interactions constituted a sizeable portion of Hedges's information exchange, monitoring, and governing activities at the school.

As she supervised students, Hedges also modeled appropriate behavior. She might, for example, pick up a piece of trash and deposit it in a container or take a food tray to the cafeteria kitchen as she reminded students of the rules, often mentioning that they should keep the school as tidy as they would their homes.

Hedges's desire to counsel students played a large part in her interactions with children, especially those who had committed some infraction of school rules. As she dealt with students she had seen misbehaving or with those sent to her for fighting, stealing, acting inappropriately in class, or failing to complete their schoolwork, she carefully listened to what they had to say about their behavior. Hedges explained this strategy in terms of her humanistic philosophy: "If you don't do something, [children] feel . . . that their problems are falling on deaf ears. I tell the staff all the time, 'You really do have to take the time out, let a child explain what happened, and be willing to at least listen, whether it's what that particular child wants, or not—it's just that someone has listened.' "

Students knew that, besides listening to their problems, Hedges would act vigorously and appropriately if they misbehaved. When infractions were serious, Hedges told students she would call their parents to report the incident. (In other instances she called parents herself, but she always followed through.) Therefore, Orchard Park's students understood that their principal was serious about discipline and true to her word.

In her dealings with problem students, Hedges implemented special plans to communicate to them that, despite their misbehavior, they were still worthy human beings and could act responsibly. In one instance, Hedges appointed the worst offenders in the school as "chair captains" and allowed them to pick their own squads to set up and take down chairs in the auditorium. The children saw this as an important and enjoyable responsibility that gave them status among their peers. In another instance, Hedges urged that a child with a particularly negative attitude toward school be assigned to the traffic detail. His teacher remarked that the boy's classroom behavior and attitude improved dramatically.

When infractions were serious, Hedges often assigned offenders work projects around the school that would contribute to the school's overall welfare. She tenaciously pursued alternatives to suspension. According to one teacher: "[Hedges] has a relationship with almost all of the children that regularly act out, the ones that are really on your blacklist. . . . If it's your child that's constantly acting out, you would almost want her to say, 'Doggone! Let's give up on that kid.' But she really never does." Hedges not only worked creatively with problem students but encouraged growing responsibility in all students at Orchard Park. For example, she taught leadership training to all members of the school's student council.

She also encouraged Orchard Park's teachers to promote positive social values in the school through classroom activities. In an unusual departure from her policy of permitting teachers to select their own classroom materials, Hedges established a schoolwide focus on her social goals by introducing a set of self-esteem materials. At the first faculty meeting of the year, she presented the materials and asked the teachers to use them as a regular part of their programs. Although she did not systematically monitor the use of those materials, her message was clear. We observed teahers using an array of esteem-building activities in their classroom, including magic circle activities, life box materials, and art projects to stimulate discussions about feelings and attitudes.

Establishing the Instructional Organization. Just as she worked to establish a positive climate, Hedges attended closely to instruction in her school. Like the other principals in the study, she directly or indirectly manipulated such important elements of the organization as scheduling, staff assignments, class size and composition, the scope and sequence of curriculums, the distribution of instructional materials, and even teaching styles.

Many of Hedges's actions (45 percent) were directed toward the organization's work structure. Most frequently, these were acts of information exchange (16 percent), followed by scheduling, allocating resources, and organizing (9 percent) and monitoring (9 percent). A less frequent but potent action was goal setting and planning (5 percent). As Hedges employed these actions to influence the work structure at Orchard Park, many of her actions involved direct contact with teachers.

On the surface, working closely with teachers about instruction seems a natural activity for principals. Research, however, shows that most teachers enjoy or expect autonomy in matters related to classroom instruction (Lortie 1975). Hedges was able to transcend this problem for two reasons. First, her own 21 years of experience as a classroom teacher and reading specialist legitimated her expertise in the eyes of her faculty. The second important ingredient to Hedges's success in influencing her staff's classroom practices was her ability to establish a culture of instruction at the school. Her emphasis on building on people's strengths and emphasizing the positive facilitated this culture. Many of her actions (7 percent) were episodes of information exchange aimed at staff relations. Experience coupled with style enabled Hedges to provide information to teachers without alienating them. Her staff regarded her as competent and nonthreatening. They not only accepted her suggestions but actively sought her advice and counsel.

While Hedges used many strategies to influence instruction both directly and indirectly at the school, the most potent and pervasive was the informal classroom visit. Hedges monitored instruction by regularly dropping in to teachers' classrooms. These visits provided opportunities to make suggestions that did not carry the onus that might accompany recommendations made after formal classroom evaluations. On many of Hedges's informal visits, she assisted teachers by working with students and by making brief, constructive, and supportive comments to her staff.

These often-repeated behaviors were key features in her strategy to reduce teachers' anxieties about her visits. She mentioned that she spent time building positive rapport with teachers before providing suggestions for changes in their instructional patterns: "I operate with the idea that we really are all a team. If I can just . . . give [the staff] enough strokes on those positives, then I can get [at] those areas that are not so well done." When Hedges made recommendations to teachers, she did so in a low-key, nonthreatening manner without embarrassing, confronting, or demeaning them. In these instances, her communication about the work structure at Orchard Park was linked with information exchange that promoted positive staff relations.

Hedges did not see herself as the only source of instructional expertise in the school. She often advised teachers to talk with their colleagues for assistance or ideas, and she organized opportunities for staff members to get together. For example, she commonly arranged for the school's reading specialist to work with a teacher to set up reading centers in a classroom or to help classroom teachers evaluate students requiring remedial help in the reading lab. The principal thus served as a "linking agent" or "information broker." Because Hedges's classrooms visits were regular, these recommendations were timely, and her staff found them helpful.

Hedges also used classroom visits as opportunities to impress on children the importance she attached to academic success. By publically complimenting students on their individual or group successes, she strengthened their self-esteem and created an ethos about learning that children would want to share. Her praise for students also carried the message to their teachers that she recognized and appreciated their work.

Principals in all schools in Orchard Park's district were instructed to formulate three-year, integrated instructional plans. Rather than viewing this mandate as unnecessary meddling on the part of the district office, Hedges saw a major opportunity to reexamine Orchard Park's instructional program with the staff and to promote the goals she held for the school and the instructional techniques she favored. Therefore, she was a central figure in every committee session scheduled to respond to the district's edict. In her nonauthoritarian style, she worked with the staff to develop the plan. She routinely recognized the value of her staff's ideas, acknowledging the positive contributions each made. Also, she promoted the ideas she wished to see incorporated into the plan. For example, she was eager to see the concept of math manipulatives included as a component of the instructional program because she believed "hands-on" experiences were necessary in a well-rounded instructional program. Through her participation in planning meetings, Hedges was able to convince the teachers to adopt this idea and include it in the overall instructional plan for the school.

Besides working on instructional plans at the school level, Hedges also participated actively in the planning of instructional programs for individual students. She attended planning meetings with teachers and parents when she knew the student involved or had a particular concern about the student's program. Several routine actions with overlapping purposes characterized her participation: information exchange and planning related to the work structure, information exchange to promote student relations, and governing the work structure at the school. In one instance, for example, Hedges reiterated the importance of incorporating math manipulatives into the regular program of instruction for a particular student. In the same meeting, she also discussed how the same teacher might help this child by using the self-esteem materials Hedges had provided at the beginning of the school year.

Hedges also involved personnel from the district office to support new instructional programs at Orchard Park and invited their opinions about issues that were important to her. For example, she discussed such long-range projects as planning a computer literacy program, establishing math centers at the school, and incorporting research on time-on-task into the coming year's staff development activities with district staff members.

These examples of Hedges's behaviors related to instruction at Orchard Park—information exchange, monitoring, and planning—illustrate her keen desire to improve the school's program rather than simply maintain it. She led her staff to confront instructional issues and to consider appropriate materials and practices that would provide more effective opportunities for students to learn.

The way Hedges allocated resources at the school also reflected her concern for improving instructional programs. A substantial allocation of resources, for example, was required to support a reading specialist at the school and the specialist's program. With the principal's approval and support, the reading specialist became a central figure at Orchard Park. The principal delegated responsibility to the specialist for conducting reading tests, assisting teachers in the development of reading centers in their classrooms, establishing individual reading programs for students who attended the reading lab, and assisting in the assignment of students to classrooms based on their reading skills. Because of the emphasis Hedges routinely assigned to reading, this specialist gained prominence in the school as another instructional leader. Teachers looked to the specialist for guidance, much as they did to Hedges.

This arrangement did not, however, always work smoothly; teachers sometimes disagreed with the specialist's decisions or, more fundamentally, with her authority. Hedges resolved one conflict by gently but firmly governing her organization: She supported her specialist's decisions about instruction and did not waver from this position. But she acted as a mediator throughout the unrest to resolve the misunderstanding—talking to teachers and the specialist to gain an understanding of their positions, then organizing a staff retreat to deal with the communications problem between the parties. Although she made a concerted effort to resolve the teachers' concerns, Hedges's support for the specialist's decisions underscored her trust in the specialist and her adherance to the principle that nothing was more important than reading instruction at Orchard Park.

Hedges also influenced the instructional organization by focusing on staff development. Hedges rewarded teachers who demonstrated interest in improving their skills. Communicating frequently with teachers, she was able to determine which teachers would be interested in inservice training as well as hear about interesting opportunities that teachers had found. Hedges allocated funds or time to these teachers so they could participate in worthwhile classes. In addition, she scheduled meetings for these teachers to share what they had learned with the rest of the faculty. She, then, extended the impact of her meager discretionary budget, providing all her staff with exposure to new ideas or materials.

Selecting and providing textbooks to classes was another type of allocation that Hedges used to influence the instructional organization at Orchard Park. She secured new math textbooks for teachers and expressed delight when teachers responded favorably to them. She arranged for the school to pilot textbooks in areas such as science and social studies. By agreeing to pilot these series for publishers, she was able to provide badly needed textbooks in two areas that suffered yearly from fiscal shortages.

Hedges's actions in the assignment of personnel in the organization— making up class lists of students and hiring staff when openings occurred— also strengthened the instructional organization at Orchard Park. At the end of the school year, when student assignments to the following year's classes were made, Hedges met with teachers, counselors, and parents when necessary. At these meetings, they discussed the child's social and academic accomplishments and needs before making class assignments. Hedges contributed her own perspectives on children's achievements, exhibiting her own familiarity with the records of many of Orchard Park's students.

Hiring teachers occurred less frequently but was no less important in shaping a well-rounded educational program at the school. During the year of our study, Hedges hired a 6th-grade teacher. To balance a very traditional 6th-grade teacher at Orchard Park, she selected a teacher with a nontraditional approach to instruction. Thus, Hedges tried to create instructional alternatives for children whenever possible. The same principle guided her decisions about which teachers would teach which grade levels at the school.

Summary. Hedges's child-centered approach to education, which emphasized the importance of a caring and nurturing environment, shaped both the structure of the school program and the operation of the organization. Our analysis has linked her routine actions to her beliefs and goals, the contextual givens at Orchard Park, and the organization of instruction at the school. An image of instructional leadership has emerged from this analysis: The principals' use of routine activities can directly influence and shape the content and nature of instruction at a school as well as the climate in which teaching and learning take place.

Hedges not only maintained order and set the conditions for instruction, as did all of our principals, but she regularly and directly involved herself in matters related to teaching and learning. The principal's actions directly affected the school's program and operation—including curriculum content, classroom organization, and teaching strategies. Hedges's success as an instructional leader was the direct result of her expertise, acquired from many years of classroom experience, and the supportive way she worked with her staff. While respecting each teacher's individuality, she built a consensus around school goals and priorities. Thus, she directly shaped Orchard Park's instructional program and still maintained her staff's feelings of autonomy and professional efficacy.

Conclusion

Based on our experiences with principals like Frances Hedges, we argue that principals can and do make a difference in their organizations' capacities to provide constructive experiences for children. The principals we worked with demonstrated their abilities to tap the wishes and resources of their communities and districts. We observed their abilities to be sensitive to the needs of their students and staffs. We found them able to create and sustain an image of what quality schooling might be and work to instill in their staffs and patrons their visions.

If principals are to act as instructional leaders, their responsibilities must lie far beyond just monitoring and evaluating didactic interactions between teachers and students. Despite many researchers' predilections to ignore this fact, the principals we worked with—and we believe many others—understand the systemic nature of instruction. Beyond technique and materials, instruction brings together students and teachers, each with different experiences and beliefs. The interactions of these individuals occur within the technical structure and social organization of the school. The school, in turn, exists within the constraints and opportunities posed by its larger context:

state and federal regulations, districtwide policies and programs, and community circumstances. Each of these factors directly or indirectly influences what happens when students and teachers come together to learn.

This broad, instructional system is dynamic. As we watched our principals in action, we also noted the uncertain environments they coped with. We watched them struggle to sustain service on dwindling budgets. We watched principals and teachers shifted between buildings as schools were closed. We documented demographic shifts that moved students in and out of schools at alarming rates; court actions that had administrators, board members, and teachers looking over their shoulders; and a changing political climate that affected the very concept of schooling.

Against this background of contextual flux, the importance of the principal as an instructional leader becomes apparent. The principal is the vital actor in the school setting who can bridge context and school, policy and program, means and ends. The principal's importance emerges from that position: He has the greatest access to the wishes and needs of teachers, students, district leaders, and parents and community members. With experience and training, the principal can formulate an image of schooling that is relevant and responsive to these groups and to begin to bring that image into being. We believe that this is exactly what our principals were about: Through their routine activities, they tried to bring to life their overarching visions while still monitoring their systems to keep those visions relevant.

Scapegoat or last great hope? In the rush to quantify excellence, to formulate effectiveness, to find the quick fix for ailing schools, principals become scapegoats. Of late, they are often held responsible for the achievement of children, one often-criticized measure of effective schooling that they have little and short-lived effects on (Rowan and Denk 1984). If, on the other hand, schooling is construed in the broader sense, they may be one of our last great hopes. Dedicated principals carry visions of quality schools into the very thick of the myriad complexities and difficulties facing schools today. Their patient routines can move their organizations inexorably toward the realization of their visions. They cannot succeed overnight. They cannot succeed alone. But they can be the wellspring that keeps all the participants in school settings pulling together.

References

Armor, D., P. Conry-Osequera, M. Cox, N. King, L. McDonnell, A. Pascal, E. Pauly, and G. Zellman. *Analysis of the School Preferred Reading Program in Selected Los Angeles Minority Schools.* Santa Monica, Calif.: Rand Corporation, 1976.

Brookover, W. B., R. J. Gigliotti, R. P. Henderson, and J. M. Schnieder. *Elementary School Social Environments and Achievement.* East Lansing, Mich.: College of Urban Development, Michigan State University, 1973.

Dwyer, D. C., G. V. Lee, B. G. Barnett, N. N. Filby, and B. Rowan. *Frances Hedges and Orchard Park Elementary School: Instructional Leadership in a Stable Urban Setting.* Report to the National Institute of Education. San Francisco: Far West Laboratory for Educational Research and Development, 1984.

Edmonds, R. "Some Schools Work and More Can." *Social Policy* 9(1979): 28–32.

Goldhammer, K. *Elementary School Principals and Their Schools.* Euguene: University of Oregon Press, 1971.

Lortie, D.C. *Schoolteacher: A Sociological Study.* Chicago: University of Chicago Press, 1975.

Martin, W. J., and D. J. Willower. "The Managerial Behavior of High School Principals." *Educational Administration Quarterly* 17(1981): 69–90.

Meyer, J. W., and B. Rowan. "The Structure of Educational Organizations. *Environments and Organizations,* edited by M. W. Meyer and associates. San Francisco: Jossey-Bass Publishers, 1978.

Morris, V. C., R. L. Crowson, C. Porter-Gehrie, and E. Hurwitz, Jr. *Principals in Action: The Reality of Managing Schools.* Columbus, Ohio: Charles E. Merrill Publishing Co., 1984.

National Commission on Excellence in Education. *A Nation at Risk: The Imperative for Educational Reform.* Washington, D.C.: U.S. Government Printing Office, 1983.

Newburg, N. A., and A. A. Glatthorn. *Instructional Leadership: Four Ethnographic Studies of Junior High School Principals.* Philadelphia: University of Pennsylvania, 1983.

Perrow, C. "Disintegrating Social Sciences." *Phi Delta Kappan* 63, 10(1983): 684–688.

Rowan, B., and C. Denk. "Management Succession, School Socioeconomic Context, and Basic Skills Achievement." *American Educational Research Journal* 21, 3(Fall 1984):517–537.

Venezky, R., and L. Winfield. *Schools that Succeed Beyond Expectations in Teaching Reading* (Technical Report No. 1). Newark, Del.: Department of Educational Studies, 1979.

Weber, G. 1971. *Inner City Children can be Taught to Read: Four Successful Schools* (Occasional paper no. 18). Washington, D.C.: Council for Basic Education, 1971.

Weick, K. E. "Educational Organizations as Loosely Coupled Systems." *Administrative Science Quarterly* 21(March 1976): 1–19.

Wynne, E. "Looking at Schools." *Phi Delta Kappan* 62(1981): 371–381.

Part II

PERSONAL PERSPECTIVES ON THE WORK OF LEADERS

4

Leadership: A Change Agent's View

John Champlin

The Johnson City Central School District in the Southern tier of New York State is today a national model of instructional excellence. The district has received extensive recognition for its outstanding student achievement and overall organizational productivity. But the district was not always so productive. In the late 1960s and early 1970s, its neighbors considered it "low man" in the area and often laughed at its efforts. In retrospect, the transformation from mediocrity to excellence is remarkable.

In April 1971, I was appointed superintendent of schools in Johnson City. I actually assumed the position July 1, 1971. It was something of a surprise. A Board of Education of an extremely conservative community sought and hired a leader publicly committed to significant school reform. The match, in fact, was not so unlikely, since the board was zealously seeking much more productivity from their schools. We met several times during the selection process. At these sessions I made it clear that I was dedicated to organizing schools around the best data and insights on how children learn. I was committed to identifying and altering existing features of school programming not consistent with those data.

Building a Perspective

The genesis of my commitment actually came about in 1965. Bob Anderson from Harvard University, who worked with Goodlad on nongraded elementary school research, served for several years as a consultant in the South Orangetown Central School District where I was an assistant superintendent for instruction. His influence slowly caused me to conclude that the existing school structure was harmful to many, ineffective for others, and only meaningful to those who would have learned anyway. I began a crusade as a "born again educator" dedicated to the idea that schools should be organized according to how we know young people learn, not according to the customary and usual dictates of convenience and ease in moving numbers of young people. That sense of mission became one of the main driving forces in my life.

During this period of rebirth, I realized the tremendous disparity between what I knew and what I needed to know if I was going to make a difference. I vowed to be an aggressive continual learner.

I recall the Charles Atlas ad depicting the evolution of a 98-pound weakling into a magnificent hulk. The attractive ads never suggested that this change required some significant discomfort and pain. The passage to competence and later expertise was never easy. Often, I avoided despair by candidly admitting what I didn't know.

Twenty years later, I am still discouraged by the profession's continued rejection of useful data. It is almost as if school leaders fear a loss of face if they were to say, "I don't know it all right now, but I'll find out, and we'll move on to make our schools better." This fear freezes schools into a hold-the-line, maintain- the-status-quo, do-only-what-I-know-now syndrome.

The central thread in my value structure was my complete and dedicated commitment to alter and perhaps even revolutionize the status quo. I was determined to live change in an unswerving and uncompromising manner, a position that served me well and carried me through the discomfort. From these deep-seated values and convictions, the Johnson City model took shape.

My position in South Orangetown allowed me to participate in creating a powerful instructional delivery system, which was awarded a $500,000 Title III NDEA grant for exemplary programs. I acquired at least five valuable lessons during this stage of my professional development that strongly influenced my later work at Johnson City.

1. Most teachers really want to do both the right and the best things. They don't because they don't know how or because they were never stimulated to discover or use existing information. Most teachers receive little encouragement to seek and inquire or grow professionally. Too many work in districts dedicated to safely maintaining existing programs. A no-wave philosophy always seems to prevail.

2. Often, principals are a much greater problem than teachers. Having attained a position of influence and authority, principals seem reluctant to accept the role of continual learner. Almost as if their egos are at stake, they become blockers. They are too busy with routines with no relationship to student success. Some even coerce staff away from any exploration that might question established routines. It doesn't take much of this type of leadership to put a permanent cap on staff interest.

3. The stimulation to grow and to continue to be an aggressive learner is purely intrinsic. Colleges, professional associations, and too often, our col-

leagues are concerned with the routines and procedures that reflect yesterday. From 1969 to 1971, I had the good fortune to be associated with an exciting, inquisitive group of doctoral students at the University of Massachusetts. During this period, I discovered *Learning for Mastery* (Bloom 1973). It had a powerful effect on me then and for years to come; it became a central theme for my view of a learning environment and a way of improving learning.

4. In the 1960s and early 1970s, change was characterized by an intense frenzy. The image of innovativeness was valued highly. Legitimate concern for sound planning and implementation was a secondary consideration. Districts publicly advertised the number and variety of new programs they had initiated. With the "Basics Are Better" movement, the overall cause of instructional change sustained an almost-fatal blow. Public resistance stiffened considerably, and teachers viewed any departure from the traditional school organization with indifference, if not outright scorn. The environment for significant redesign became more nonsupportive, often bordering on the hostile.

Despite the tone of the times, my goal to reorganize a school based on the way children learn remained unaltered. The behavioral sciences and the insightful reporters of successful change projects stressed certain factors that needed to be managed singly and in concert if change was to occur and be successful. I identified seven critical factors in my doctoral research project (Champlin 1970):

- The creation of a supporting, enabling environment;
- The presence of clear, attainable goals that are publicized and constantly in use;
- The presence of a change agent who can effectively break the equilibrium holding an organization in place;
- The use of a systematic, planned process that is open and subject to alteration;
- The involvement of the community as an active partner and participant in any major change;
- The presence of effective leadership with vision, a sense of mission, a goodly measure of courage, and a sense of the importance of followers; and
- A commitment to renewal that disallows compromising for lesser attainments and always aspires to higher levels of sophistication.

5. The more success South Orangetown experienced and the more attention and recognition it received, the more indifference or hostility it drew from colleagues in the area. It was almost as if they wished for our failure because it might justify their nonproductive programming. This understanding was important to my personal survival in Johnson City. When Johnson City emerged from the depths of a do-nothing, low-man image, I expected it to cause our neighbors great pain. When we received neither

encouragement nor tacit support, I was not surprised. Because we knew what to expect, we built a strong internal support system for sustenance. We developed pride in our entrepreneurship.

Indifference to Johnson City's success was not just a local, parochial issue. Our State Department of Education seemed to find us an embarrassment. We were succeeding while they didn't even seem to be asking the right questions. Field experience proves that school improvement can be most productively expedited through state-supported networking. Within such a framework, districts will support and build on each other, constantly delighting in the success of others. We have a considerable distance to go in developing this network.

What I brought to Johnson City was a distillation of some critical experiences and an approach toward organizing schools that guided my tenure there. I did not go to Johnson City in search of answers; I went with a clear vision of what might be and a determined dedication to bring it about.

The Johnson City Years

I have selected ten critical areas as significant to the Johnson City story. My intent is to convey a flavor of the strategies and leadership decisions that had the most impact on the district's long-term success. I do not mean to imply that these were the only important factors or that there were cause-and-effect reactions. These are, however, the "musts" in any successful school improvement plan.

Establish Expectations

I actually became involved in Johnson City three months before I became superintendent. I knew I had to make inroads and to establish my expectations and intentions as early as possible. I have never accepted the prevailing contention of taking a year to get established on new turf before moving ahead. I believe the leader must communicate the values and priorities that will be a basis for later action as quickly as possible, so the followers can learn what to expect. I have always wondered how leaders rationalize instructional mediocrity for an extended period of time before finally declaring an intent to modify existing efforts.

I thought the professional staff should hear the same message I had shared with the Board of Education during the selection interviews. My message was direct and clear: I do not come to maintain your current program because it is substantially ineffective. It contradicts what we know about how young people learn best. Although I was diplomatic, the staff learned that I intended to take appropriate risks to effect program improvement. Business as usual was no longer acceptable. I offered no specific substitute program; I established a need to create a school environment far more consistent with the best available learning data. At this point, I introduced two terms critical to my value and belief system: *goal driven* and *data driven.*

The term *goal driven* conveyed the intention that every professional action or decision worked toward our published goal: all students learning well what schools taught. It was a constant reminder of our singleness of purpose and our intention to achieve it. The goal statements were derived from a research base—*data driven.*

The early reactions to both terms were largely negative. Eventually, both terms had a powerful impact because we constantly insisted on their integrity and their value. Both represented a new venture into professionalism, a theme we used frequently. These terms challenged our staff to be practicing professionals by making decisions consistent with the best available data. At first, many bristled at the notion that they were less than practicing professionals, but they later agreed that the terms focused their professional actions and activities on data rather than on feelings.

Influence the Community

When I took the job in Johnson City, I accepted the need not only to deal aggressively with the professional staff but also to reeducate, renorm, and reactivate the entire community. The community's views of education were vintage 1920. Only the fortunate escaped the assembly lines of the Endicott-Johnson shoe factory or the more modern confines of IBM. Bright girls went to work in banks, and lucky boys from families with some means might make it to college. A strain of conservatism and a suspicion of anything different from yesterday contributed to the need for substantial intervention if we were to raise the sights of the community.

I learned early in my career that, to avoid immediate conflict and negative response, school patrons must be involved in the change. The literature of the 1960s told many stories of innovators who had ignored this prerequisite and soon found themselves engulfed in community strife.

About six months after I began in Johnson City, I asked the Board of Education to authorize the creation of a community task force on school excellence. Key citizens, parents, members of the professional staff, and students served on this task force. Its purpose was to consider what we knew about learning, the process of instruction, and education as a critical societal function.

Six task force sessions were scheduled, with topics including the purpose of education research, school improvement, and exemplary program models at the elementary and secondary levels. We carefully chose consultants, selecting only known experts. They were all willing to emphasize that school excellence could be attained if the community and staff reached for it together. Each two-hour session contained one hour of information and a second hour of discussion. Questions focusing on the main points of the evening's presentation were prepared and distributed. The key question was What does this information mean to the Johnson City schools?

The six weeks went remarkably well. The community and staff were never put down for past programs, yet they began to see an optimum that we could attain. The vigor of the community residents serving on the task force stimulated the professional staff who previously had felt that the community had no real interest changing the schools.

The task force recommendation, quickly enacted into policy by the Board of Education, committed the district to becoming data driven and to constantly aspiring to better insights and higher levels of performance. It was a bold and courageous step for the board to take, considering the community's past views of school and the nature of learning. To my knowledge, this public policy was the first of this nature in the country.

The policy became a powerful weapon. It enabled me to initiate a much larger purpose and mission. In all fairness, the staff had made the accurate assessment that many of the district residents had no interest in any change that might affect their taxes. I was chastised for aspiring to a "Cadillac" when the community was content with a "used Ford." Such observations failed to diminish my hopes. Publicly, I stressed that the district's children needed the most productive learning opportunities possible. I repeated the task force recommendations that our schools use research and make the best practices part of our instructional delivery system.

Privately, I was driven by my conviction and dedication to create a school organization capable of producing sustained excellence. My doggedness caused some to view me as stubborn and strong-willed. In retrospect, their view was probably accurate (and consistent with being goal driven). Had I wavered on anything I espoused as being important, I would have been seen as being "able to be had."

Ensure Readiness

Thoughtful management ensures successful initiation and institutionalization of change. An important management concern is readiness for any planned improvement effort. At Johnson City, we needed time to demonstrate a need, to legitimate a response, to recruit support, to train teachers, to internalize values, to problem solve, and to grow and mature. We weren't looking for a quick fix. We planned carefully and immersed ourselves in a readiness phase.

The first step was to establish a successful living model in our district, one staffed with home-grown teachers and populated by garden-variety kids. As a demonstration center for our goal-driven model, we selected a moderately sized elementary unit. In an elementary school, there is less territory to defend. The basic elementary school is child-centered without the secondary school's concern for standards or content.

We took time to sort out the real values and commitments of those who professed readiness. I wanted no one in our demonstration school without the "gut" desire to be there. I had seen too many people bail out in "innovative" districts when the kitchen got hot and it became the vogue to claim they didn't really want to be there anyway.

Eight teachers from the Oakdale School, a K–6 school unit, volunteered to participate in some preliminary explorations. After these, they would have the right to say "go" or "no." The eight teachers went with me to South Orangetown (where I still worked) for a three-day visit. During this visit, they enlarged their appetites for "things that might be in Johnson City." They also began to know me, both personally and professionally. As they left, I urged them to consider involving themselves in intensive training so that we could create a model capable of producing new opportunities for their pupils back in Johnson City.

After only a few days, the team informed me of their enthusiasm and their dedication to be a part of this adventure. Their willingness to volunteer removed all hints of coercion and produced instant ownership. In effect, they had dedicated themselves to this project. This critical breakthrough also established a level of expectation months before I officially became superintendent of the district.

In September, when I was on board, we started the training cycle. I provided the initial training in brief after-school sessions and half-day released time blocks. Seeing their superintendent roll up his sleeves and actually work with them in training and problem solving was a totally new and stimulating experience for these teachers. It established my credibility in terms of technical expertise. The district no longer had to go outside for consultant assistance. We had in-house power. The combination of released time and after-school time for training gave teachers and management the opportunity to invest something in the experience. The teachers and I agreed that we would contribute equally so that each would have something at stake. The training began in a spirit of cooperativeness and mutuality.

The training progressed smoothly to the total satisfaction of all involved. The actual school program "converted" on February 1 without incident and with almost instant success. Taking the time to get ready paid rich dividends. The Oakdale experience, as it became known, established the pace and the theme for the rest of our redesign activities.

The Oakdale program validated the planning and stimulated the involvement of others. While the Oakdale staff was in training, readiness sessions were being conducted in three additional elementary schools and in both secondary buildings. The three elementary school staffs received intensive summer training during July 1972. All three made successful entry in September 1972.

The key to success was the professional staff. At Johnson City, staff members were neither encouraged nor permitted to move into the program until they were ready. Extensive training and demonstrated skill were prerequisites. We never moved beyond our capacity to supervise, support, and coach those who crossed the line into the new program. Because the stakes were high, I spent at least two hours daily at Oakdale. This project warranted my time far more than office routines. Central office support, in any form, was available.

Restructure the Role of the Teacher

One of the primary targets in the Johnson City redesign effort was breaking the stereotype of the teacher role. Our intent was to create a far more compelling role, a stimulating role that would allow more professional decision-making autonomy. Our preentry training established new expectations about the quality of teacher decision making, introduced the mastery learning instructional process, and built the necessary skills demanded by mastery. Teachers worked as teams. This approach required strong daily coordination and articulation, and it forged a new working bond between teachers and principals, one based on expanded new roles and enhanced decision-making. The program required far more extensive teacher participation in decision making than the traditional hierarchial setting afforded.

The staff members needed time to gain a realistic perspective on their behavior. They perceived their existing level of professional performance as much higher and much more sophisticated than it actually was. This misperception is a form of protective self-hypnosis. We want to believe we are doing the right thing; in the absence of clear, objective feedback about our performance, we reassure ourselves about our high productivity.

Each staff member had the time and opportunity to personally "own" a pressing need for program improvement. Each was guided through four phases of personal development: the acquisition of information and facts, the creation of understanding, the opportunity for guided application (including feedback and coaching), and the creative application of new skills.

The training sessions provided two valuable types of input to staff. The first was an opportunity to think through and create a written philosophical premise that would establish a reason for all our instructional decision making. Mindless behavior, enacted and perpetuated without rationale or reason, was eliminated. Second, specific training was provided in every skill the new program required. The staff development efforts recognized that adult learners need frequent opportunities to acquire and practice new skills. Our persistence in gaining a data base through the literature and then focusing comparison of the data base with our actual performance paid off.

The staff identified problems. No school practice, procedure, policy, or tradition was exempt from scrutiny and subsequent alteration if it was inconsistent with our resolve to become data driven. This bold commitment persuaded the staff that we meant what we said about unfettered reform.

Problems that emerged from an analysis of daily practice were subjected to a standard problem-solving procedure. Consensus solutions were sought. Unsolved issues were recycled in the search for a more appropriate alternative. Thus, the program was not immobilized by small problems, and the staff could do whatever was necessary for success.

We succeeded in breaking down what I described as the "self-contaminated classroom." It took some time and considerable dialogue over what was possible if and when teachers developed collaborative skills in planning, executing, and renewing. We knew from previous experiences that to expect teachers to work together successfully without specific training in the associated skills was unwise. This approach was invaluable in reducing the tension and apprehension associated with facing new or different challenges. This accomplishment was not easy in a district where teachers had traditionally closed their doors in the morning and operated as they wished for the rest of the day. A team-teaching model emerged only after extensive training on how to relate and work together.

Reshape the Role of the Principal

Principals in Johnson City, not unlike their counterparts all over the nation, had for decades operated from a position of line authority and positional power. Control was tight. Teachers had little decision-making autonomy—usually only if they boldly usurped minor privileges. From the beginning, one of my major tasks was to reconstitute relationships so that teachers gained a sense of power and influence. I wanted to give teachers a strong sense of importance by making it possible for them to exercise professional judgement and to make important decisions that enhanced student learning. This sense of importance was critical to stimulating their ownership.

At first, principals found altering long-standing behavior difficult, even though they intellectually accepted the need to encourage teacher independence. I began by retraining principals the second day I joined the district and never wavered from strenuously monitoring their transformation. Congruent with being data driven, principals delved deeply into the existing literature on authority, influence, and leadership. We emphasized that leadership influences followers toward the attainment and ownership of goals; it does not coerce and mandate follower behavior.

During work periods with principals, the role of the principal as instructional leader was described. The role was to enable the staff to close the gap between what might be and what was actually in place. Eventually, the principals understood that they were freed when teachers dealt independently and skillfully with issues and problems. As long as teachers remained within the boundaries of making decisions on the basis of the best available data, prevailing educational philosophy, and our overall commitment to success, their freedom to make decisions should be respected.

Besides time and patience, stronger persuasion was occasionally needed to alter the principals' behavior. The process was eased by openly exploring new roles that were created collaboratively. We reached open, practically unanimous agreement. We provided feedback to each other on how new roles were being played. I frequently monitored these interchanges. While not all the principals moved away from their previous roles with grace and willingness, they did eventually work successfully to assume the role of instructional leader. As the entire staff became more accustomed to exercising decision-making responsibility, our program grew, and the staff members took more pleasure in their professional growth.

Articulate the Vision

In everything I did during the early years in Johnson City, I modeled my beliefs and dedication in every way possible. I wanted the staff to see me work toward making my stated vision a practical reality. I took every opportunity to train, work with, and support teachers. I advocated new roles and then allowed the staff to see me practice what I urged them to adopt. I modeled the behavior and took the risks. It was obvious this direction would produce conflict, particularly as new practices clashed with traditional procedures. In each contact with staff, I tried to be consistent in what I advocated in living the values I espoused.

Peters and Waterman's *In Search of Excellence* (1982) stresses that leadership means a sense of vision and a commitment to a basic mission. Our experience in Johnson City validates this observation.

Develop a State of Continuing Renewal

In large part, the Johnson City project was successful because we never permitted ourselves to reach a point where we were satisfied with what we had accomplished. We constantly introduced new refinements at staff development sessions. For example, Johnson and Johnson, from the University of Minnesota, did some especially powerful research on the impact of peer learning teams. We immediately embraced and incorporated their ideas in our program, with great success. In addition, team and building staffs periodically reviewed their progress toward goals they had established or toward performance standards created by the district. After assessing progress, they quickly established new strategies. We kept each other on our toes by constantly pressing to get into new issues. At times, some thought the pressure was unfair, but the feeling was short-lived. The Administrative Council took real pride in the currency of chosen issues.

I was propelled by the belief that effective learning or, in the case of our staff, effective behavior modification, takes place on the edge of personal frustration. I insisted on uninterrupted activity for fear that once we relented, the energy to start up again would be far more exhausting than that required to maintain our effort. Frequently, principals pleaded for a respite for themselves and their staff. We went through a time when they believed they could only do one new thing at a time. But I insisted that we address a number of issues concurrently, although I acknowledged that equal vigor would not be given to all. To have done otherwise would have diminished the pace of development to a point of ineffectiveness. The staff finally accepted the concept of juggling a series of issues, but only with continuing persistence on my part. They eventually appreciated my insistence on their continual growth. They recognized that, had I backed off, they would have, too.

Create an Opportunity for Self-Esteem

While our paramount goal was significant student success, we constantly sought an accompanying sense of teacher success. It seems an oversimplification to note that, in large measure, this goal was accomplished by focusing on enhancing student success. As pupils became more successful, teachers took satisfaction in recognizing that their amended behavior contributed to the success. Pupil success and greatly expanded staff enthusiasm were contagious.

I took every opportunity to publicly praise our staff members for their commitment to professionalism and for their dedication to helping more children learn well. We generated an intense district pride in our supportive school practices and in our willingness to address and resolve tough issues about learning. As we gained national recognition, the staff took great corporate pride in their progress. They were especially proud of the considerable distance they had moved from the behavior of their peers in neighboring districts. I frankly encouraged this pride and took every opportunity to recognize their success publicly.

As the word of our substantial success spread, we were invited to make presentations at more meetings and conventions. I always took groups of teachers with me to participate in the presentations. These meetings were an opportunity to give public testimony to what the teachers were doing and to stimulate their ownership. The personal satisfaction our people gained from numerous audience comments added significantly to their self-esteem.

The design of our staff development program was another important aspect of developing personal esteem. We trained one person from each team who in turn trained her colleagues. It is a challenge to have the responsibility for providing opportunity for peer growth. Because each teacher took a turn, each had the opportunity to confront the challenge. A sense of camaraderie and significance soon followed.

As we matured, our willingness to give teachers the freedom to make important decisions about time, corrective teaching strategies, and varied groupings paid rich dividends. Everyone realized that this freedom was the epitome of true professionalism. Reinforced by their realization that their decisions were respected and never second-guessed, teams eventually sought out creative alternatives and implemented them with skill. Freedom and responsibility became powerful motivators. Our people were practicing professionals.

Control Change

Schools have generally ignored the accumulated knowledge about organization behavior, individual needs and the management of change. Experiences of schools in the 1960s provided powerful lessons: The well-intentioned but haphazard insertion of programs as if they were interchangeable parts was a fatal miscalculation. The literature on systems theory clearly indicates that any change in one subsystem produces accompanying changes in other subsystems.

Interventions in Johnson City were predicated on the assumption that any intervention or alteration would have an eventual, if not immediate, total organizational impact. This understanding allowed us to be proactive in anticipating and planning. A holistic, systems approach enabled us to avoid small single-phased changes that might have splintered efforts. The term *synergism* has special meaning here: The sum total of several small efforts does not equal the effect of a single, totally comprehensive effort. Our commitment was to make a total impact by anticipating all affected areas and then making adjustments to produce compatibility and reciprocal support.

For example, we had a serious relationship problem to correct. The Board of Education had taken some delight in keeping teachers' salaries at the lowest possible level. A staff that felt its basic needs were not being met was not likely to venture into an activity requiring extra effort and commitment. After some negotiation, the Board moved district salaries somewhat above the county median. The raise was a significant signal to the staff, and energies moved from complaining to focusing on instructional improvement.

Our long-term plan had four phases: establishing a staff development program, developing entry-level skills, operating the program, and evaluating and renewing. Specific steps in one phase enabled movement to the next phase. The plan was systematic and thorough. Everyone knew what to expect and what was expected of them. Our intent was to avoid surprises and to be prepared to handle contingencies that might develop. Our success within this process reassured the staff members, who soon believed that change was possible, not something to be feared.

We worked with the community as well. Parents needed a chance to express their concerns, so we scheduled small group meetings with eight to ten parents. Our intent was to avoid large group meetings that prohibit participation and inhibit understanding. Large groups frequently serve as a forum for dissidents with a speech to make. One of our most successful strategies was to identify and isolate possible irritants in a small group. Our premise was that their contamination of others like themselves would not hurt us at all, although the opposite would be true if we mixed them with other positive, interested parents. The strategy worked. We kept rescheduling appointments until we captured over 90 percent of a school's parent group. We talked in understandable terms, strenuously avoiding "educationese," asking the community to give us a chance to succeed. Teachers, not administrators, conducted these sessions. Eventually, we had a broad base of parent support.

The change-agent function is an especially critical one. The person who fills this role needs considerable authority and power as well as abundant ego strength. We managed change; we were not paralyzed by it. Everything we did was intentional. Our proactive posture was far more comfortable and reassuring than a reactive, responding role.

Insist on Organizational Excellence

I also strived to change the value structure of our school organization so that revised beliefs, attitudes, and relationships would be socialized in to the organization. I wanted the staff's commitment to what we achieved to be so strong that, even if I left, the program would continue. I have now been away from the district for four years; the total program is alive, well, and even better.

This success was possible for many reasons. The effort to build a new culture by putting our beliefs, practices, and values into written documents and policies that we constantly used as a basis for renewal and growth was crucial. We purged former practices as quickly as possible by replacing them first in working documents and soon after in monitored practices.

In Retrospect

The Johnson City plan succeeded for several reasons:

1. We committed to being data driven; we never wavered. We purged ineffective practices.

2. We committed to being goal driven. Everything we did contributed to what we sought to create.

3. We committed to renewal, always correcting and adjusting. The ability to adjust took away the pressure to be right all the time. We were not afraid to take risks.

4. We used the available knowledge on change and behavioral management to plan and control every move we made.

5. We developed an intolerance for mediocrity, both personally and organizationally. We converted to professionalism because there was no other way to achieve our goal.

6. We trained staff members in every skill we asked them to perform. We encouraged their creativity in using the skills.

7. We won the community as an ally because we worked with them and gave them reason to support us.

8. We won our staff support by creating a strong sense of need, ownership, and commitment.

9. We never rested. We always renewed.

10. Despite pressures, leadership never lost sight of the goal.

The Johnson City experience is unique for many reasons. It was successful in an era when so many other ventures were failing. The initial prognosis for success was nil.

As a change agent, it was my task to influence and alter the existing organizational equilibrium while holding the organization together. At first, my activities were not received with joy or enthusiasm. Many people in the early days were comfortable with the status quo; they saw no need to change. The lethargy and resistance inherent in the staid, never previously challenged organization quickly became hostility and resentment toward "the new guy" who dared to challenge the way it always was and, in the view of many, the way it would always be.

A former elementary art supervisor depicted me in caricature as Don Quixote battling the traditional windmill, the intractibility of the Johnson City system. Once, I was the target of the union "hit squad" who decided that since I couldn't be had, I had to be gotten. Board members were elected to "get me"; there was a close call only once when my contract was renewed by a narrow 4 to 3 vote.

I survived in Johnson City because of my deep commitment to our mission and the strong support group of several key administrators who came to the district with me. Leadership is lonely even with strong colleague support. During one hot spring conflict, my children kept asking me, "Daddy, are we going to move again?" The agonies of leadership are not contained in one's office.

Frank Sinatra sings a popular melody, "I Did It My Way." That, in large measure, describes Johnson City, a vision carefully conceived, thoughtfully managed, and doggedly sustained. I pursued my vision of making school a happy, healthy, achieving place for students and staff. Indicators of success such as higher achieving graduates, greater employability of students, community involvement, staff maturity, and ownership evolved.

References

Bloom, B. *Learning for Mastery*. Washington, D.C.: College/University Press, 1973.

Champlin, J. R. "A Study and Analysis of the Utilization and Influences of Change in the Schools of Concord, Mass., 1965–1970." Doctoral diss., University of Massachusetts, Amherst.

Johnson, D. W., and R. Johnson, eds. "Social Interdependence in the Classroom: Cooperation, Competition, and Individualism." *Journal of Research and Development in Education* 12, 1 (1978): 1–52.

Peters, T. J., and R. H. Waterman. *In Search of Excellence*. New York: Harper and Row, 1982.

5

Leadership: A Woman's View

June E. Gabler

Well, tonight's the night! I'm going to my first public interview for the superintendency of a new school district. My pulse is a bit high but really nothing to worry about. I've been a superintendent for ten years, and I've done my homework on this system.

This evening I arrive home promptly at 5:00 P.M. to feed the family. As I place dinner on the table, I silently bless the inventor of the automatic oven for making the meal a breeze to prepare. The kids and husband are all on their best behavior and dinner is over quickly. Everyone is doing their best to make the meal pleasant and quick so I can be on my way. The kids volunteer to do the dishes while I change. As I dress, I conjure up the faces and names of the seven Board of Education members who will be conducting the interview.

I drive for an hour and a half, arriving for the interview 15 minutes early—time to catch my breath and relax before entering the building. The search committee chair greets me in the hall and ushers me into a large instructional media center. The board members are standing around a large, U-shaped table on one side of the room. The audience faces them from the opposite side of the room. The chairs are arranged in long rows that seem to go on forever; each chair is filled.

The chair escorts me to the board table and introduces me to each board member. I mentally note my gratitude to the person who thoughtfully included a brochure with the names and pictures of board members in the material sent me. I recognize each one, which immediately puts me at ease. As I'm being introduced, I notice a lone chair sitting between the board table and the audience. I experience a sinking feeling as I realize that I am to sit there—in the middle of nowhere—with my back to the audience and my face to the board. As I'm being led to that chair, I try to imagine a way of responding gracefully with one of the groups always behind me.

The board president pounds his gavel and announces that the interview is to begin. He proceeds to introduce me to the public. While I'm marshaling my opening remarks, I realize that the president has concluded and is now talking to me. He is remarking on my appearance. For the next several minutes, he explains to us all that I do not fulfill his expectations of a female superintendent. He had expected that I would be large, raw-boned, and clumsy. A female superintendent, he proposes, has to look and act "tough, masculine, and callous" to gain the respect of the students, staff, and community.

Angry, embarrassed, and smarting from his negative and belittling comments, I fight for composure. I tell myself to chalk off the introduction and focus on the task of interviewing in a capable and professional manner.

The questions cluster, for the most part, around finance, negotiations, and school law. Finally, the board president closes the interview by again explaining how I have failed to meet his expectations as a female superintendent. While I'm talking informally with a few board members and people from the audience, the board president's wife walks up and asks in a loud, skeptical voice, "You don't really believe a woman can be a successful superintendent in a school district like this, do you?" I look at her in astonishment and answer in a somewhat exasperated tone, "Yes, I do! As a matter of fact, I know a female superintendent who is doing an excellent job in a district much like this one." She looks shocked and questions, "Oh, really! Who is she?" "Me," I respond. With that as my final comment, I turn sharply and walk out of the building, accompanied by the search team chair.

During the drive home, the debriefing is short, if not sweet. I feel confident that my answers to questions were appropriate and knowledgeable, but given the president's frustrated expectations, it's evident that I'll not be back for a second interview. Well, so much for equal employment opportunity. I am disappointed at my reception but find it less difficult to understand the board president's attitude than to accept his wife's unspoken assumptions.

The next day, an apologetic search committee chair calls. He is exasperated with the board for allowing the president to start the interview on such a destructive note. He says he was especially disappointed in the silence of the female board members. He sees their silence as tacit agreement with the president's assumptions about female superintendents. He explains that the search team had taken great pains to explore the "equal access" issue. The board members had assured the team of their unqualified intent to employ the "best superintendent" for their district, regardless of gender, color, or creed. During our conversation, it becomes evident that what board members say about "equal access" at times can differ widely from what they do about it.

The search committee chair concludes with his suspicion that the board members had not really expected the search team to include a female superintendent as one of the top finalists. During the interview, their expectation that there would *not* be a qualified woman became a self-fulfilling prophecy.

Several days later, I receive a copy of the newspaper account of the interview. The female reporter chose to ignore the president's inappropriate remarks, but she dedicated a great deal of ink to my answers to the board's questions. She commented on how thoroughly I answered the questions, especially in the areas of finance and negotiations, and added, precisely on cue, the three tellale words—"for a woman."

Why Me?

An experience such as this can stimulate extensive thought and profound soul searching. Perhaps I should be accustomed to these experiences after 30-odd years as a female administrator, but I still find them unnerving and distasteful. I tend to review each episode again and again in a frustrating attempt to discover answers to the same hard, painful questions: What did I do wrong? Do other superintendents face these same kinds of experiences? Why was I singled out for such an unpleasant experience?

In reexamining the events of the opening interview, it's evident that I didn't meet the expectations of the board president or his wife. Ordinarily, the first response of people whose expectations are violated is to ignore the mismatch and preserve the expectations. But in an interview situation, it is difficult to ignore the interviewee. Consequently, one must go further—to defend the violated expectation. In this case, I did not look like a superintendent. By inference, if I did not look like one, I would not perform like one. When extended questioning suggested that nevertheless I might be capable, there was a fall-back defense: Who would want an "unusual" (read "queer") woman at the head of their district?

My reflections on this experience have led me to recognize a point that has helped me place my career frustrations in perspective. I have concluded that the last thing people will do is to change their ill-informed expectations in the light of the new evidence I present.

Why was I singled out? Because I'm a female educator who deliberately chose to practice my skills and knowledge in a traditionally male-dominated career, that of a school superintendent. Why me? Because I don't fit the expectations of most of the staff, students, parents, and community. Where did I go wrong? By expecting those with whom I work with to ignore the myths of gender bias. Do other superintendents face these same kinds of experiences? Yes, if they are female superintendents.

In our society, people are reluctant to accept women as leaders. Consider the image of women that has dominated our movie and television screens. Recall the typical western, with its male hero planning, organizing, directing, and controlling the defense of his passive little woman whose children clutch her skirts.

Given such views of women, there is little wonder that men were hired as the leaders of educational institutions. Even now, after years of proselytizing, equal employment opportunities are slim in the public schools of our nation. In July 1985, the *Executive Educator* reported:

- 95.8 percent of all superintendents are men;
- 91.1 percent of all top central office administrators are men;
- 93.4 percent of all secondary school principals are men; and
- 81.1 percent of all elementary school principals are men.

In fact, negative reaction appears to be growing to the enforcement of equal opportunity from those meeting more competition and reduced opportunities. It would be naive not to expect a backlash. Women now are filling administrative positions in sufficient numbers to be viewed as a threat to some male incumbents.

On the other hand, many decision makers have looked at the task to be done and have hired the most qualified candidate. They have done so in sympathy with sound, well-informed professional principles. I credit them with much of the progress that women have made to date.

As I travel across America, the questions I am asked reinforce my conviction that ill-informed expectations are the core problem facing female administrators. This problem is gender bias. It has many forms, as the questions demonstrate. Over the years, evidence has mounted in support of certain answers.

What Are the Unique Problems Facing Female Administrators?

Female administrators face unique problems. Their socialization causes them to question their ability to lead. In addition, the belief that they must excel in everything they tackle—while balancing a career, schooling, and family responsibilities—tends to become an extremely heavy burden. The prejudices they meet, the stereotyping they experience, and the discrimination they encounter in hiring and promotion erode confidence and even hope.

Now, however, enough successful female administrators fill advanced positions to provide those moving through the ranks with new insight on the problems they will confront. The aspiring female leader has resources unknown to her female forerunner. Help is available in such areas as career goal setting, resume writing, interview techniques, communication skills, public relations methods, and discovering the real rules of the game. Also available is sage personal advice distilled from those with experience. For instance, it is acceptable to say no when requested to do the impossible at work or at home, to understand that it's normal to fail or fall short of excellence occasionally. Now, the aspiring female administrator can more easily marshal resources for blending career, school, and work into an integrated life-style. Yet all this assistance may still fail to illuminate the underlying problem that is hidden more often in the eyes of the beholder than in the skills of the aspirant.

Given abundant skill, the female school administrator must still convince students, staff, parents, community members, peers, and Board of Education members that she can lead. "So what?" someone will say. "The male aspirant faced the same task." This assertion, as far as it goes, is true. But the big and often unnoted difference lies in the expectations of all the significant others. The expectation for the male administrator is overwhelmingly that he *will* succeed. The expectation for the female administrator, at best, is the hope that she might.

The successful woman is seen as unusual if she is able to provide sound leadership to an institution or organization. This exceptional status tends to lead the significant others in the institution to focus disproportionately on the female administrator herself rather than on the job or task to be performed. This focus is debilitating and difficult to overcome. To deflect the focus of the system from gender to task, the female administrator must devote much energy.

Unfortunately for women, even after expending the considerable extra energy required, the rewards of overcoming negative expectations are never as great as those gained in simply meeting positive ones. Commonly, a man, surrounded by positive expectations, succeeds as an administrator despite marginal performance. The energy he expends can go directly to administrative tasks rather than to the job of overcoming a gender bias. A woman administrator expends considerable time and effort convincing significant others in her work world that she is a capable and competent leader. She must prove herself over and over again in each new administrative position and in each new institutional and organizational setting.

Why Don't Women Want to Work for Women?

Our society has done a good job of teaching women to compete against one another in subtle ways. Hidden and unhealthy competition among women spawns jealousy and envy. It prevents women from being team players and from supporting one another. It causes them to perceive that behavior is excellent when employed by a male administrator but objectionable when employed by a female administrator. While he is seen as an aggressive administrator, she is described as a pushy woman. If women view leaders of their own gender in this fashion, can women really be shocked and angry when men do the same?

Why Don't Men Want to Work for Women?

Often, when an administrative position is open in a school district, a few male teachers and administrators observe that they hope they don't end up working for a woman. These people have usually never worked for a female administrator. The occasional one who has worked for a woman or who has a friend with a female boss will reluctantly admit that the experience was a good one. Then, they hastily add that she, of course, was an unusually fine woman and administrator, implying that the odds are overwhelmingly against finding another good female boss.

In probing for reasons, I have often uncovered a strong supposition that any female superior would most likely be pushy, picky, bitchy, temperamental, prejudiced, power-mad, and secretive. However, studies conducted over the last ten years on female administrators and their leadership styles have shown that colleagues tend to describe female leaders as well-organized, caring, considerate, and effective (Lueder 1983).

Why Do Some Male Colleagues Have Trouble Relating to Women?

Some men are not comfortable working with women as their colleagues. They simply do not know how to develop a working relationship with a woman, particularly if she is a peer or superior. They have had no previous experience.

For example, my husband and I, along with several of his university colleagues, were attending a conference. As we drove to the conference, I noticed one of the new members of the group, a man, struggling to converse with me. His difficulty was noticeable because the rest of us had attended this conference together before and were quite comfortable with one another. I watched him explore alternatives in his attempt to find a comfortable way to relate to me. He tried and then discarded the approaches he would use in communicating with his own wife, the wife of a friend, or his grandmother. Never once was he able to relate to me as a colleague.

During the conference, we did not see each other until we entered the station wagon to drive home. He asked if we might sit together to talk. Surprised, I asked why he would want to talk to me. He then described his inability to accept me or any other woman as a colleague. He had ignored all his female peers at the university by discounting them as professional equals. His wife was a professional woman, and she had decried his refusal to relate in a meaningful way to either her work or to her colleagues. He claimed he had been drawn up short when I would not allow him to relate to me except as a colleague. It had bothered him to the point that he sought out professional women at the conference to learn how to relate to them as colleagues.

He said it had been a painful struggle for him to put aside his prejudices and accept these women as equals, but that he had gained in the process.

Why Is It Lonelier for a Female Administrator Than a Male?

To some degree, an administrative position is inherently lonely. Being a female administrator is more so. Being a female superintendent is possibly the loneliest position of all.

I still remember my worst year—my first administrative post as elementary principal. On Friday, I was a kindergarten teacher, well-liked and respected by my peers, the school administration, students, parents, and the community. On Monday, I began as principal. The friendships with so many of my teacher colleagues faded; they were no longer comfortable with me. The students, parents, and community became more negative about me and my performance. I was shocked, hurt, and humiliated by the cosmic change of attitude. I couldn't understand it. I hadn't changed; why had our relationship changed?

It took me a year to understand what had happened. People's perceptions of me had changed from that of colleague, teacher, and friend to that of boss, evaluator, and enforcer of rules. While the support I had was fading, I sought to build a new network. It took a year to gain the trust and respect of my new fellow administrators.

It was a difficult and lonely year, but it taught me a valuable lesson about developing and being a part of a support network. I learned to make certain that I am always available to any colleagues who may need me. Someone out there might be as lonely as I was that first year. I've learned to overcome my shyness, to pick up the phone and call other superintendents who may be equally shy or reluctant. More important, I've stopped being hurt when I'm not included in a lunch or dinner invitation at conferences. I'm not bashful. If it's important, I'll do the inviting.

Why Aren't There More Female Superintendents Now That There Are More Female Board Members?

In 1985, 36.1 percent of all board members in this country were women, a greater percentage than ever before (*School Board News*, 1986). Yet these women who have worked so hard to be elected in their home districts are often the same ones who tell the superintendent search teams that they are not interested in interviewing female candidates. The reason commonly given by these female board members is that they don't believe a woman can administer a school district as ably as a male colleague. Isn't it odd that women continue to be their own worst enemy. By refusing, on the basis of gender, to allow a Search Team to include a qualified candidate, these board members deny equal access to jobs for all women, themselves included.

Why Don't Mothers in the Community Support the Female School Administrator?

Some communities have a "mothers' mafia" (Messinger 1983), a small group of attractive, bright mothers who are either unemployed or under-employed. These women have talked for years about doing something different, about getting a college degree or a job, but one thing or another has always managed to get in the way. When a female administrator is employed in the district, she becomes a target of this group, especially if the administrative position is highly visible. One might think these mothers would be delighted to see a woman succeed in a leadership position, since it might mean increased access for their daughters in the future. Not so. Instead, the mothers perceive the female administrator as a goad and a recrimination. She represents the sacrifice not made, the goal unachieved. If the female administrator is happily married and has children as well, the personal attacks on her are likely to be even more determined and vicious. For these community women, the female administrator demonstrates what harder work and less comfort might have gained. Often, their goal is to quietly undermine the female administrator. Should she manage some success in spite of their efforts, they usually buckle down and try harder.

Why Don't Women Educators Get the Same Encouragement to Enter Administration as Men?

When I consider the time and energy women have spent trying to overcome the barriers preventing them from entering the field of administration, and when I compare this situation with the encouragement and support that men have received, I am astounded and somewhat angered. Men and women paid the same tuition and service fees to the universities. The workloads were equal, if not increased for the woman. But the services received were not equal. When I studied for my doctorate, so few women were in the program that the informal support of a study group was also unavailable.

I remember the orientation on the first day of classes when I began my doctoral program. As a part of his preliminary remarks, the dean told the group that if any of us were female (there were 49 men and me), we might just as well drop out now. First, he did not expect that female candidates would make it through the program. Second, if one did happen to get through, it was highly doubtful that any school district or educational institution would employ a woman.

After the orientation, I walked up to the dean and said, "Dean, please take a good look at my face because I want you to recognize me when you award me a doctorate. I'm going to be one of the best students you've ever had in this university. I also want you to know that there is a school district where they hire female administrators—it's the one in which I now work."

To his credit, when he handed me my degree, the dean remembered my challenging statement. He told me that he had been watching my progress and that he wished me well in my career.

Today universities need students, so women in doctoral programs are becoming more acceptable. Furthermore, women prove to be good students. Unfortunately, some universities are still not providing comparable place-ment services to both men and women seeking administrative positions.

Why Isn't the "Old Girls" Network as Effective as the "Old Boys" Network?

Until recently, the "old girls" did not know how the "old boys" network operated. Women didn't know they needed to have a network to capture a top-level position in an institution or organization. They thought that all it took was hard work; eventually the organization would recognize worth and promote able people. Women now know that, besides hard work and lots of skill, the move to the top requires a supportive network.

As yet, the "old girls" network is too sparse and thin to assist many women to top positions. The few women in top positions have barely begun to help those coming up behind. I think Judith E. Palmer's writing (1979) about women's awareness of equity issues helps explain, but not justify, the behavior of today's top women. Palmer describes the five stages of growth in women's awareness.

The first stage is *curiosity*. The woman is curious but feels that she is not part of the movement because she has never really experienced sexual discrimination. In the second stage, *identification*, the woman sees a connec-tion between her own experience and the discrimination other women have suffered. *Anger* is next. Recognizing that she has suffered discrimination, the woman is furious. Unfortunately, some women become stuck in this stage, and their anger slowly destroys or cripples their careers and personal lives. Stage four is *consolidation*. The woman consolidates her energies into per-sonal goal setting and works actively with other women to influence the institution or organization. The fifth and final stage, according to Palmer, is *personal power*. At this point, the woman reenters the organization or institu-tion as a competitor.

But this scheme needs a sixth stage, which occurs when a woman who has reached a power position in the system extends herself to facilitate the progress of other competent women. This behavior is inherently *professional*. In the professional stage, the woman who has arrived works consciously to ensure a continuous flow of able new talent for the future. The "old boys" give the professional stage its due with their network, and there is no reason that "old girls" cannot do the same. Ultimately, of course, it should be an "old peoples" network. Some of the "old boys" are ahead of us already in moving toward that objective.

Few women in top leadership positions have reached this sixth stage. Perhaps they have to expend all their energy maintaining their own positions. Many young female educators are moving through the administrative ranks and are asking for help from the "old girls," but only a few are finding a willing female mentor.

Why Should Women Want to Belong to
Male Service Clubs?

Because some male service clubs restrict membership, female leaders are denied access to an important segment of the community. They are deprived of a direct line of communication with the "movers and shakers" of the business and professional community. They are prevented from developing an easy familiarity with the power structure of the community. During the club meetings, informal dialogue about countless issues takes place; problems are often solved before they become a source of polarization. Worthwhile friendships and support networks are formed; these can be critical to a school administrator—especially a superintendent. All these advantages of an active membership in a service club are denied a woman. In addition, most of the professional men in the community never develop a first-name acquaintance with a female leader in a social setting.

Why Are Female Administrators Attacked More
Frequently by the News Media?

A female administrator always interests the news media. In the minds of some news reporters and commentators, the very fact that female administrators are in the minority makes what they do noteworthy. Since negative news items always attract more readers, the media are quick to note a negative slant or a hint of scandal. In some cases, their own biases are the basis for the story.

Two summers ago, a newspaper reporter called for an interview about the closing of two elementary schools in our district. When he arrived for the interview, he began by commenting about the car I drove. Apparently, my slightly sporty car did not fit his idea of a female superintendent's vehicle. The interview went downhill from there. Each of his questions checked out another of his perceptions. The next day, I was not surprised when a hatchet job appeared on the front page. The article dealt with me personally, giving little information on the closing of the elementary schools. Courses in several universities now use this article as an example of the kind of press a female superintendent might have to weather because of her gender.

Why Are There Communication Problems?

Over the years, I've noticed that men and women have a somewhat different sense of humor. At times, I find male humor unkind, because men will joke about something that is distasteful or about a person's problems. I've come to realize that men use humor to tell a person that they are concerned about him without exhibiting what might be misconstrued as feminine sentiment. But this masculine expression of concern may hurt their more sensitive colleagues. I've adjusted my humor to accommodate these exchanges somewhat, but I also protest and protect an individual when it is too biting.

I became aware of this difference in humor by accident as I walked into a superintendents' meeting many years ago. I met a fellow superintendent on the way in and noticed his hesitation at joining the meeting. I asked him if something was wrong. He said the ridicule and snide remarks he expected about the problem he was experiencing in his school district were almost more than he could face. The problem had been reported on the front page of that morning's newspaper. He went on to say that he had not slept the night before because of the prospect of this morning's meeting. In my naive way, I told him there was nothing to worry about because I was sure the others would be sensitive to his problem. I was wrong. The jabs and harsh comments started immediately. I expected them to die down in a few minutes, but, again, I was wrong. Finally, I said, "Look, instead of making jokes, let's sit here and discuss the problem. With our collective thinking, we ought to be smart enough to solve the problem. Let's remember, one of us could be sitting in the same chair next meeting." The laughing ceased. The troubled superintendent received support, we found a solution. For me, that meeting was the beginning of fine relationships and lasting friendships—the product, I think, of a healthy blend of masculine humor and feminine compassion.

Do Women Lead Differently Than Men?

Leaders employ different styles. In fact, the same leader may vary style to suit situations. Most leaders, however, tend to gravitate to a predictable style. While it seems clear that personality characteristics influence style, the role of gender, if any, is not at all clear at this point.

Lueder (1983) at Tennessee State University has used the Myers-Briggs Type Indicator Instrument discussed by Pat Guild in Chapter 6 to investigate the leadership styles of the "Top 100" educational administrators chosen each year by the *Executive Educator*. When Lueder compared this population's characteristics with the "normal" population of school administrators, he found a significantly higher number of extraverted, intuiting, thinking, judging personality types. The women responding in this group were especially strong in these characteristics.

Leaders with such characteristics tends to be enthusiastic innovators. They actively strive to understand people and often achieve an uncanny knowledge of what makes others tick. They sense and adapt to other people's needs in social interaction. They tend to be objective, logical, and matter-of-fact; others sometimes read them as lacking in personal warmth. Fairness, openness, and consistency characterize their behavior; others know immediately what is expected and where they stand. In fact, Lueder (1983) described this leader as a "visionary," a type significantly different from the normative school administrator. Lueder's findings suggest that, while a proportionately higher number of female executives share this profile, they do not differ significantly in leadership style from the men in the successful group.

What Can a Woman Do?

Given the evidence of considerable gender bias in educational administration, what can a woman do? She can recognize the situation and develop strategies to confront it. These strategies are not gender biased; they will work for men in administration, too.

Find time to socialize. A few minutes of relaxed conversation with colleagues over a drink or a cup of coffee makes the job of managing easier because others see you as a human being. In addition, hidden agendas that fester in the work settings often emerge at these times.

Take time to smile. You and your family need to become comfortable living in a "goldfish bowl." All school leaders are a focus of interest for a community, but the focus is sharper on the female administrator. Learn to be yourself and to enjoy yourself in spite of the watchful eye of the community. Occasionally, you must be a good actress to succeed.

Make the effort to communicate. Appear in all the news media: district, community, and staff newsletters; the student newspaper; radio and television stations. Get your side of the story to the public, staff, and students. If necessary, use letters to the editor. Work hard at building a rapport with the editors of the newspapers, the owners of the radio stations, and the managers of the cable television companies. If you don't project your own voice, others will invent one for you.

Play tough. Don't be afraid to play "hard ball" when necessary. Be prepared to call in a "chit" that someone owes you. Earn the respect of the community power structure. When something needs to be done because it is good for the district and for you as the leader of the district, play the game and plan to win.

Lose gracefully. There are times when you are not going to win the game. Take defeat, failure, disappointment, discouragement, embarrassment, bungling, incompetency, mismanagement, and criticism with grace and finesse. It's a skill that's crucial to all leaders.

Take risks. Risk taking is a legitimate leadership skill. The key to developing this skill is learning to "figure the odds." Use your analytical strengths and intuition to guide you. Learn as much as possible about the political ramifications of the risk, but then move on with the task in spite of them. Don't be afraid to take risks.

Exhibit poise. Never show your nervousness. Regardless of the situation, keep your chin up and your brain working. Be a perfect picture of poise, at least on the outside.

Be visible. A smart leader does her managing by walking around, by being visible to the staff, the public, and the students. What gets done by employees is what gets supervised. Supervision demands that the administrator is on the move and can be expected at any moment.

Be competent. Make certain that you stay knowledgeable by reading and studying the professional journals, by attending conferences, and by continuing your formal education. Female administrators must exhibit knowledge in finance, negotiations, law, and care of facilities, since people suppose that women know little in these areas.

Conquer with kindness. Get to know each member of the "mothers' mafia" personally. Search them out at social events. A smile, a hello, a handshake, and a kind word sometimes throw the enemy off guard. They may prompt a reevaluation or even a conversion. If you refuse to be intimidated and, instead, appear at ease, you are more likely to win the battle.

Share. Share your knowledge and skills with others in the profession. The sharing helps others to grow. It is, perhaps, the most natural sign of the leader.

Give credit and feedback. Find ways to compliment the staff in public for work well done. On the other hand, find ways to discuss shortcomings openly and frankly in private. It may not be pleasant, but overlooking staff shortcomings is a sure sign of administrative incompetence. Be certain to provide concrete suggestions for improving performance.

Be a guest. Have a staff member or friend invite you at least once a year to be his guest at each of the service clubs in your community. Make sure that you are asked to present a program about the schools at each of the clubs at least every other year. Since you cannot be a full-fledged member, this contact allows you to build a communication network on an informal basis with the active business and professional men in the community.

Exhibit leadership. Bring a sound leadership style to the institution. Focus on the four management functions of planning, organizing, directing, and controlling. Forget about wanting to be liked. Concentrate on the administrative tasks. Try to put others at ease, and then apply just enough guidance to help them develop on the job. Enjoy the advancement of staff members as you would your own. It's a true compliment to the administration of a district when other districts hire at a higher level the personnel whose skill you helped to develop. Direct others by taking a personal interest in their aspirations and by harnessing them when possible for the good of the district. Evaluate yourself periodically, and include others in the process so you can view your performance through their eyes.

Communicate in the system. A superintendent must be especially careful to maintain open communications with Board of Education members. If there is "sunshine law" requiring that board meetings be open to the public, arrange small-group private meetings with the board members. Visit each school or classroom at least once a year. I like to have lunch with students at each of the schools and, when possible, to take the board members along.

Conclusion

The core problem female administrators face is ill-informed expectations. Despite the emphasis here on the stumbling blocks, I take joy in my work and am happy in my career. I've learned a female administrator can even turn her gender into an asset. We female administrators can choose to merely survive the negative expectations of others or to overcome them with flair and a Cheshire cat grin. I hope my female readers will choose the latter course. Then, I expect them to share their experiences to help others gain insight.

References

Lueder, Donald C. "Personality Profiles of the Top 100 Educators." Unpublished paper. Nashville: Tennessee State University, 1983.

Messinger, M. H. "The 'Mafia Mothers': Another Peril Facing the Women Principals?" *Executive Educator* (August 1983).

Palmer, Judith D. "Stages of Women's Awareness." *Social Change: Ideas and Application.* 9,1 (1979): 1–4. (Bethal, Mass.: NTL Institute.)

School Board News. "Fewer Women Minorities on School Boards." January 22, 1986.

Part III

PERSPECTIVES ON THE DEVELOPMENT OF LEADERS

6

How Leaders' Minds Work

Pat Burke Guild

The giraffe is an animal often associated with leadership—leaders are willing to stick their necks out! For many years, I've collected giraffes. I took a few to a seminar that I recently conducted on leadership for people in banking. As I showed them several giraffes, I asked them to describe the leadership qualities that each giraffe evoked. The first giraffe, a plain wooden figure with clean lines, inspired people to comment that a leader is strong, solid, and willing to stand firm. Another was made of different-colored straw, and this giraffe reminded them that a leader is often unpredictable, innovative, and exciting. A third giraffe was a cookie cutter; people commented that a leader should be open. A fourth giraffe was made of rubber, and it suggested that a leader should be flexible. The fifth, a small porcelain figure, prompted the comment that leaders need to handle situations delicately and subtly. Still another giraffe was on rollers; people commented that leaders should get around and cause things to move.

After we talked about ten different giraffes and generated a long list of admired qualities of leadership, I asked people to rank order the three qualities most important to them. Setting priorities was, and is, not easy. Often, we expect strong leaders to have all the qualities on the list. Yet realistically we know that effective leaders, leaders we admire, have different characteristics. They show their leadership skills in individual ways.

Research confirms the giraffe analogy. The recent reviews of effective leadership, especially from the effective-schools research, have confirmed this commonsense notion. While studies indicate that effective educational institutions have strong leaders, the qualities and characteristics identifying a strong leader are not clear. "We found no single image or simple formula for successful instructional leadership," Dwyer reported (1984, 33) in a three-year study of successful instructional leaders by the Far West Laboratory for Educational Research and Development.

In a five-year study at the University of Texas at Austin, Rutherford (1985) reported five essential qualities of effective principals: having a vision, identifying goals, creating a supportive climate, monitoring progress, and intervening appropriately. Then he asked whether effective leaders were all alike. "The answer is both yes and no. Yes, effective school leaders will demonstrate the five essential qualities of leadership in their work. But no, they will not demonstrate these qualities through identical day-to-day behaviors" (p. 34).

Don Lueder (1958/86) reported a review of the literature on leadership traits: "The studies failed to support the . . . assumption that a person must possess certain traits in order to be a successful leader" (p. 58).

In some ways, this finding, frequently cited in the literature, is frustrating. But it also an exciting and liberating conclusion that allows leadership to emerge in different ways for different people.

Given any set of criteria or list of qualities, experienced leaders, as well as less seasoned ones, will identify to a greater or lesser extent with certain aspects of leadership. Our perspectives on what behavior identifies a good leader are different.

Leadership Competencies and Individual Characteristics

While perspectives differ, leaders share some common denominators, usually specific competencies. Good leaders are organized, for example. But "effective organization" can mean neat, complete files to one person and an effective management team structure to another. Good leaders have good human relations skills, but some are friendly, gregarious, and outgoing, while others operate more behind the scenes, supporting people by their attention to tasks. The examples could go on—effective leaders in education should have some common basic competencies, but they exhibit these skills in different ways.

The distinction between personal characteristics and leadership competencies is important. While effective leaders do have certain competencies, they also have a personal style. What causes these individual differences? What makes one person behave, and therefore exhibit leadership skills, in one way, while another person acts differently when dealing with a similar leadership task?

Cognitive Style and Individual Differences

Many psychologists agree that the most fundamental basis for human behavior is perception and the perspective that perception brings to our actions. When I "see" the world, specific situations, and people in certain ways, I respond in a way that makes sense to me. For example, if I'm the type of person who sees things exactly and literally as they are, my behavior will reflect that kind of perception. On the other hand, if I'm the kind of person who reads between the lines, who sees intentions and meanings, my behavior will reflect those perceptions. Consider how two people with different perceptions see budgeting. The leader who focuses on a situation in a literal manner will probably want specific budget categories for various expenditures. The leader who seeks general meaning is often more comfortable and effective with fewer broad-based budget areas.

In everyday terms, most of us recall times when we attended the same movie with friends and yet saw very different things. Or we witnessed and reported a car accident, only to find out later that another witness reported the event in a very different way. Neither impaired eyesight nor untrustworthiness causes these discrepancies. Rather, each of our experiences are filtered by a much more important quality—the cognitive process of the mind.

Several researchers have described differences in perception. Witkin and Goodenough (1981), cognitive-style researchers, discussed the difference between field-dependent and field-independent perception, akin to the difference between seeing the forest or the trees. Management professor David Kolb (1984) and learning-style researcher Anthony Gregorc (1982) both described the difference between abstract, symbolic perception and concrete, realistic perception. These qualities of the mind govern not only what the eye sees but also what the ear hears and, of course, what the heart feels. Cognitive style, then, determines the message that is received from a situation, the personal meaning that we form. This perception and processing becomes the guide for individual behavior.

Jung's Psychological Types

Perhaps the most influential researcher in this area was the Swiss psychologist Carl Jung, who described cognitive roots of human behavior in his 1921 book, *Psychological Types*. Jung identified two distinct and opposite kinds of perception. Some people depend on their senses to give them accurate, exact, careful information from the environment. *Sensation* makes people appreciate literal meaning, detail, and exact recall. At the opposite end of the continuum, some depend on reading between the lines, understanding nuances, seeking meaning, and looking for possibilities. *Intuition* makes people appreciate the subtlety of messages, the intention as well as the words, and the relativeness of understanding (see fig. 6.1).

In a 1983 article, "A Look at How Managers' Minds Work," John Slocum and Don Hellriegel discussed the behavioral manifestations in management tasks for people who depend on either sensation or intuition for their

---

Figure 6.1   Jung's Psychological Types

PERCEPTION:

Sensation
Facts
Practical
Details
Present

Intuition
Possibilities
Imaginative
Patterns
Future

JUDGMENT:

Thinking
Objective
Justice
Analyze
Head

Feeling
Subjective
Harmony
Empathize
Heart

---

perceptions. "Sensing" managers break information down into small bits containing hard facts. They work all the way through a problem to reach a conclusion. They show patience with repeated details. These managers tend to be good at precision work; they dislike new problems unless there are standard ways to solve them. The "intuitive" manager loves solving new problems, is impatient with routine details, jumps to conclusions, and dislikes taking time for precision. While the sensing manager appreciates stability, the intuitive person is suffocated by stable conditions. He seeks out and creates new possibilities, often to the dismay of a sensing colleague who sees things going quite well the way they are.

Another important dimension that Jung described to explain human behavior was the different ways people make judgments. Some people decide with their heads and pride themselves on being logical, rational, calm, cool, collected, and objective about decision making. Others make decisions with their hearts. They pride themselves on their sensitivities, their perceptions, their understandings, and their ability to see how decisions affect the people involved. Jung labeled objective decision making as the *thinking* process and subjective decision making as the *feeling* process (see fig. 6.1.)

Again, Slocum and Hellriegel (1983) gave some examples of how these qualities affect management behaviors. "Feeling" managers are aware of other people and their feelings. They tend to be sympathetic and relate well to most people. They like harmony and need praise themselves. "Thinking" managers, on the other hand, are generally unemotional. They base their decisions on external data and generally acceptable ideas and values. Since they can carefully solve a problem by considering a variety of alternatives, they tend to be good planners.

Cognitive Style and Leadership

The notion of these individual differences in perception and judgment is, of course, not new (Guild and Garger 1985). Whether we use Jung's vocabulary or someone else's words, the significance of these differences has been accepted for a long time. But to what extent is understanding these cognitive-style differences important in understanding leadership?

There are two implications. The first is that self-awareness is important in the development of leadership abilities. The second is that leaders must work effectively with people with different cognitive characteristics (see fig. 6.2).

Self Awareness—Understanding My Cognitive Self

When I am conscious of my own processes of perception and thinking, I'm in a better position to use my strengths. In Jung's terminology, for instance, people with sensing perception need to understand their strengths in dealing with reality, in being able to see a situation practically, and in having the ability to make quick decisions. People with the intuitive perception need to recognize their ability to focus on long-range goals, to find new ways to solve old problems, to deal with nuances, and to understand the complexities of situations. Self-awareness helps people articulate their strengths and use them for effective action.

By the same token, effective leaders are aware of their limitations and understand the need of both complementing personal strengths with skills of colleagues and compensating for limitations through some specific actions. Leaders with a strong sensing style must often deliberately seek another's perspective on the long-range consequences of their actions. Strong intuitive leaders may need to find reliable people to attend to immediate, practical problems. The ability to maturely accept that I can't do everything and be

---

Figure 6.2 Implications of Understanding Cognitive Style

SELF-AWARENESS	WORKING WITH OTHERS
Using my strengths	Understanding my impact on others
Compensating for my limitations	Acknowledging others' contributions
Understanding my perspective on decision making	Identifying others' needs
Planning professional growth	Using others' strengths
Controlling my stress	Flexing my style

---

everything to everybody is a quality of effective leaders. Recognizing this reality in terms of natural cognitive style brings balance and depth to our view of the world.

Self-awareness of cognitive style can also help me to understand why I make certain decisions and why I place certain values on specific tasks as an educator. Recognizing that the hundreds of small and large decisions that I make every day are often natural reflections of my own perspectives can help me to understand why I take the directions that I do and why other people don't always agree. If I understand the importance of the effect of individual perspectives on behavior, then I'll also realize that it is often futile to argue for the one right way to do something or to bicker with somebody over whether her way or my way is best. While *best* judgments can be made in certain situations, very often the *better* or the *best* depends on the perspective of the decision maker.

For example, if I see a discipline policy as tangible evidence of an administrator in control of the building, it may be my sensing perception that's valuing the concrete and specific nature of a written discipline code. By the same token, if I place a high priority on bringing artists and musicians into my building even though I may not be able to measure the immediate results of such efforts, this priority may be a reflection of my own intuitive style that leads me to believe and "just know" that these experiences are valuable.

Another important implication of cognitive-style self-awareness is planning for professional growth. Planning for growth implies both understanding my areas of need and having the ability to develop ways to improve my skills. Intuitive people, for example, are not helped by advice to forget their dreams and deal with one day at a time. Instead, leaders with an intuitive style must be encouraged to dream but also to bring their dreams to fruition by setting priorities and following through with action. Instead of cutting off the dreams of the intuitor at an early stage by expecting immediate action, an attitude of "Let's work this idea through to see how we can implement it" brings greater professional growth. Often, the task yields better results as well.

Finally, self-awareness of cognitive style enables a person to understand and control stress. Leaders in education cannot escape the pressures and tensions that come from external situations and from the fast pace of the job. But how each leader handles those pressures will result in more or less personal stress. If I identify my problem areas, I have a better handle on how to control or avoid them. This self-awareness can be extremely important in my development as a leader. For example, a leader with a strong thinking style needs enough time to collect appropriate and accurate data. Decisions that have to be made quickly are stressful. In this case, self-awareness can help the strong thinking leader recognize that not everyone involved in the decision is going to need the same completeness of data that he needs. A leader with a strong thinking style can also conclude that she needs to put more effort into anticipating upcoming decisions and to start ahead of time. Still another appropriate adjustment would be for the thinker to recognize his tendency for additional stress by anger at other people's last-minute, off-the-cuff demands. These demands reflect after all, only one person's perception, often a result of the perceiver's discomfort with a lack of thinking time.

Certainly, any leadership role involves stress. But the ability to control it and to work productively through it is one of the key qualities of effective leaders.

Sensitivity to Others—How They Think

The second implication of cognitive-style knowledge is its application to the many facets of leadership that require working with others. When I recognize diversity, I can appreciate and use it and be able to "style-flex" to create "win-win" situations.

An important first step is knowing my own impact on others. For example, while I may see myself as thorough, careful, and attentive to detail, someone else may see exactly the same behavior as petty and rigid. While I may see myself as creative, enthusiastic, and a long-range planner, someone else may see me as impractical, a daydreamer, and careless. Being aware of the potential impact I have on others can be an extremely important quality in working effectively with other people.

By the same token, when I understand others, I see their strengths and also their needs. A colleague or subordinate who is extremely good with detail and with analytical and objective decision making needs the time to focus on detail and to collect the data she bases her decisions on. Successfully working with that person requires anticipating these needs and allowing the necessary time and access to data. It also means not asking for immediate, quick decisions but rather planning ahead and stating the deadlines for major projects.

Another implication for working with others is that effective leaders must use the strengths of other people. This ability means appreciating diversity in a positive way. It means expressing that appreciation publically so that everyone celebrates the personal differences of colleagues rather than being exasperated by them. When I put the appreciation of diversity into action, it means consciously forming committees so people of different cognitive styles play important roles. Thus, a final decision will include practical aspects, long-range visions, a rational analysis of data, and a consideration of the human impact of the decision.

Finally, an effective leader is motivated to and has the skills to "style-flex"—to temporarily modify behavior to create a "win-win" situation. We all recognize times when we've been able to adjust our own behavior in a relationship with another person and have seen the resulting communication as productive and positive for both of us. We've found a common ground; we've clarified mutual purposes. We've been patient and we've avoided creating a conflict. This relationship worked because we genuinely wanted to work with others. Knowledge of cognitive style, especially the understanding of my impact on others and their needs, can bring more sophistication to the skills of style-flexing.

Impact of Cognitive Style on Education Leadership

Cognitive-style differences affect several aspects of leadership (see fig. 6.3). Perhaps the first and most important is the sense of vision, purpose, and mission that the leader holds. What is the purpose of schooling? What place does the school play in the community? What is my best vision of an institution? What do I want most to have happen for students when they leave my school? These and other questions concern the ultimate purpose and mission of the school. My cognitive style, my perspective, will influence my answers to these questions.

A sensing cognitive style, a practical perspective, will help me to look directly at the reality of the job market and seek ways for students to acquire the necessary skills. The long-range focus of an intuitive perspective will cause me to look at the meaning of learning and to emphasize creating a love of learning for students. A thinking cognitive style will help me focus on intellectual knowledge and skills. A feeling trait is likely to concentrate my attention on educating "the whole child."

Another area of leadership difference is interpersonal relationships and communication. A strong thinking cognitive style will cause me to stress clear, articulate, accurate, and unemotional communication, both in person and in

---

Figure 6.3   Impact of Cognitive Style on Leadership

1. VISION: purpose of schooling

2. INTERPERSONAL RELATIONSHIPS: communication, team building, group dynamics

3. ADMINISTRATION: management priorities, delegation, problem solving, time use, public relations

4. CHANGE

5. MOTIVATION AND SUPERVISION: personnel decisions, staff monitoring, coaching and evaluation, conflict resolution

6. DEFINITION OF LEADERSHIP

---

writing. My memorandums will be specific; they will attend directly to the situation and state messages objectively. A feeling judgment style will cause me to be more subjective in my oral and written communications. I will consider the impact of what's being said on the individual people receiving the message. I will pay more attention to the perspectives of the people who listen to me. For example, I'd be more likely to check a sensitive memorandum with a few trusted staff members before sending it out to all staff. I'd be more likely to deliver messages in person so that my tone of voice and my nonverbal cues aid in transmitting the message. These differences in communication patterns will show up in a variety of leadership behaviors, especially in situations involving group dynamics such as team building and staff morale.

The way I manage and administer the programs in the school will also reflect my particular cognitive perspective. Whether I spend more time with people, with ideas, or with task completion reflects my cognitive-style traits. The things that distract me—interruptions from people seeking my attention or my own need to review data and recheck something also indicate differences in perspective.

An ability to delegate jobs and decision-making power to other people also reflects a particular management perspective. Am I willing to share an idea, get people going on it, and then step out? Am I going to supervise the completion of a task so that I can be sure it is finished to my satisfaction? Am I going to require a careful plan before I let someone be responsible for a job? Am I going to delegate to certain people because I trust them?

What priorities do I set? Is it more important to spend time with the staff and with the community? Is it more important to keep up with recent educational trends and curriculum research? Is it more important to see that the building or the district facilities are managed appropriately?

What about the area of change? Do I initiate it actively and enthusiastically? Do I bring people on board early in the change process? Do I follow the initiatives of my staff or my colleagues in making changes? A leader with a strong thinking cognitive pattern is likely to initiate change only after it has been carefully considered and shown to work in other situations. A leader with a strong sensing pattern is likely to initiate change after identifying an efficient and effective way to solve a problem. Strong intuitive-style leaders often propel change to keep people fresh and to keep new ideas moving into the district. They have a tremendous faith, intuitively, of course, that the change will bring positive results. For leaders with a strong feeling pattern, change is a group process. The ideas about and the actual direction of the change are much less important than the enthusiastic involvement of the staff in the process.

Myers and McCaulley (1985) examined data that identified the cognitive styles of more than 1,000 school administrators. They determined that nearly

30 percent of elementary and secondary principals have a sensing/thinking cognitive-style pattern, one focusing on everyday issues and careful, detailed planning of tasks. Change administered by these leaders is likely to be slow and cautious. In recent studies (1987) Lueder examined the cognitive style patterns of 100 top educators and 100 educators to watch identified by *The Executive Educator.* In both groups he found that over 35 percent had an intuitive/thinking pattern, indicating a preference for innovation and perhaps explaining their national recognition.

In the leadership task of supervising, motivating, influencing, and evaluating the staff, the perspectives of my cognitive style also have clear implications. A leader with strong sensing style is likely to supervise and evaluate people with an emphasis on the end result. She looks, for example, at the achievement scores of students in a classroom to measure the effectiveness of the teachers. She also looks at the achievement scores for a school as a whole to measure the effectiveness of the principal. She motivates and mobilizes her staff to produce a tangible product by requiring, for example, that they have a school improvement plan with specific actions and timelines associated with each objective.

A strong intuiting administrator evaluates on the basis of the inspiration that teachers offer to students and principals give to teachers. He values the teacher's efforts to bring local artists into the school. He is pleased with the staff's enthusiasm for the PTA fund-raising drive to purchase computers for the classrooms. When it comes to motivating staff members, he seeks to inspire them by addressing the long-range consequences of education and by talking about the tremendous potential of the human mind.

Finally, how do I see leadership? Is a leader a good manager? Is a leader someone who inspires? Do I see the effective leader as the behind-the-scenes organizer, planner, and mover? Is the effective leader the active, out-in-front carrier of the flag? Do I see an effective leader as the catalyst who mobilizes other people to action? Do I value the leader who sets direction by making specific content recommendations and mobilizing resources to implement those particular decisions? The way I see the role of leader reflects my cognitive style.

Issues and Subtleties

Cognitive style is a complex concept, and its relationship to leadership is not simple. Jung and subsequent style researchers have explained that all effective people can operate from different perspectives depending on the requirements of situations. However, these researchers believe that each person develops preferences and strengths more in certain patterns than others. This idea is analogous to writing with a preferred hand. If I am right-handed, I can certainly perform with my left hand, but the quality of the work decreases, even though I concentrate and exert more effort.

Successive research studies have shown that cognitive style is a neutral trait. It is not better to have a sensing or intuitive perspective in perception, or a feeling or thinking attitude toward judgments. My style is simply the way I am. Success depends on the effective use of my style and on the appropriate adaptation of behavior to the situations. This information suggests that effective leadership skills are developed by focusing on strengths. The studies on qualities of effective leadership cited earlier in the chapter have confirmed this personal aspect of effective leadership.

It is also true that people behave with a combination of traits. Jung believed that each person has a perceptual preference (sensing or intuition) and a judging preference (thinking or feeling). The combination and intensity of these functions leads to a tremendous variety in human behavior. There are not four simple patterns. In addition, Jung talked about attitudes toward the external world (extraversion) and attitudes toward the internal world (introverson). These dimensions again add complexity to the basic four functions and help explain the uniqueness of each human being.

The terms leadership style and management style have also been used in a variety of ways. Sometimes the reference is to specific behaviors without regard for the roots of the behavior. For example, one person may have an autocratic leadership style, which may describe a specific set of response behaviors. When the word style is used in this way, it is often akin to describing competencies of leadership—a hierarchy of skills is established. Thus it is "better" to have a certain leadership style, just as it is better to have more leadership skills.

Cognitive style, with its focus on understanding the roots of behaviors, is a more fundamental notion than, for example, situational leadership theory as described by Hersey and Blanchard (1977). Their focus is on responding appropriately to the needs of a situation and developing a range of task- and people-oriented behaviors to be able to do that. Their theory is a useful way of applying insights from cognitive style knowledge by helping each individual recognize what leadership skills might be most important to develop and practice. Cognitive style theory would explain the basic leadership approach one might take, and situational leadership theory would argue for conscious use of specific behaviors appropriate to the immediate situation.

Leadership Style

Effective educational leaders are special people. They have competencies in a variety of areas. But if we focus on a specific competency, such as the ability to deal successfully with people, we recognize that it is possible to deal effectively with people from the perspective of different cognitive styles. The feelers deal effectively with people because of the sensitivities and perceptions they bring about people. The thinkers deal effectively with people because of their ability to be straightforward and direct. The intuitors deal effectively with people because of their ability to inspire and excite people. The sensors deal well with people because of their ability to mobilize people to get the job done. While specific leadership competencies can be identified, different leaders will exhibit these skills differently.

Therefore, when each one of us works on our own leadership development by studying the theories, the research, and the experience of effective leaders, we should also consider our own individual cognitive-style characteristics. Each of us needs to be aware that our own cognitive pattern influences our assimilation of theory and experience. We incorporate into our lives the aspects that seem meaningful to us. We develop our own leadership skills, at least in part, on the basis of our cognitive pattern. Recognizing our own uniqueness is a distinct asset as we develop our leadership style.

Knowledge of cognitive style doesn't prescribe how to be an effective leader, nor does it automatically bring new behaviors, qualities, or competencies to leadership. It brings an approach to understanding, with more wisdom, the notion of leadership. It is an approach that recognizes as its core the reality, the importance, and the tremendous value of individual differences.

References

Dwyer, D.C. "The Search for Instructional Leadership: Routines and Subtleties in the Principal's Role." *Educational Leadership* 41 (February 1984): 32–37.

Gregorc, A. F. *An Adult's Guide to Style.* Maynard, Mass.: Gabriel Systems, Inc., 1982.

Guild, P.B., and S. Garger. *Marching to Different Drummers.* Alexandria, Va.: Association for Supervision and Curriculum Development, 1985.

Hersey, P., and K.H. Blanchard. *Management of Organizational Behavior: Utilizing Human Resources,* 3rd ed. Englewood Cliffs, N.J.: Prentice Hall, Inc., 1977.

Jung, C.G. *Psychological Types.* Princeton, N.J.: Princeton University Press, 1971. (Revision by R.F.C. Hull of translation by H.G. Baynes. Originally published in German by Rascher Verlag, Zurich, 1921.)

Kolb, D.A. *Experiential Learning.* Englewood Cliffs, N.J.: Prentice Hall, Inc., 1984.

Lueder, D.C. "The Trait Theory Revisited: Principals; Personalities and Perceived Leadership Behavior." *National Forum of Educational Administration and Supervision* 21, 2 (1985/86): 58–67.

Lueder, D.C. "Psychological Types and Leadership Styles of the 100 Top Executive Educators in North America." *Journal of Psychological Types* 12 (1987).

Myers, I.B., and M.H. McCaulley. *Manual: A Guide to the Development and Use of the Myers-Briggs Type Indicator.* Palo Alto, Calif.: Consulting Psychologists Press, 1985.

Rutherford, W.L. "School Principals as Effective Leaders." *Phi Delta Kappan* 67 (1985): 31–34.

Slocum, Jr., J.W., and D. Hellriegel. "A Look at How Managers' Minds Work." *Business Horizons* (1983): 58–68.

Witkin, H.A., and D.R. Goodenough. *Cognitive Styles: Essence and Origins.* New York: International Universities Press, Inc., 1981.

7

Vision and the Work Life of Educational Leaders

Linda Tinelli Sheive
Marian Beauchamp Schoenheit

Recently, the term *vision* has appeared consistently in discussions of school leadership. Before Blumberg and Greenfield's (1979) research on effective principals and Peters and Waterman's (1982) research on excellent organizations, few discussions of leadership included the term. Now, the notions of leadership and vision are closely associated. An ASCD (1985) videotape, *The Effective Principal*, lists having a vision as one of five essential features of effective school leaders. Robert Cole, in his editorial in the September 1985 issue of *The Kappan*, defines leadership as "articulating a vision."

Of course, the concept that some leaders are guided by a vision of a preferred future is widely accepted. Frequently, we have asked groups of educators to name visionary leaders, and the responses have come quickly: Martin Luther King, Gandhi, Joan of Arc, John F. Kennedy, Mother Teresa, Hitler.

But the vision of educational leaders and the visionary leadership of great political figures differ. We don't expect effective principals or superintendents to take on the stature of a Gandhi or a Martin Luther King. What, then, does vision mean in the context of the work life of educators? Do all school leaders have a vision? If they do, where does it come from? What impact, if any, does a vision have on the career of a school administrator?

We conducted a research project to answer these questions. We gathered our data by interviewing 12 New York State educators who were identified by a rigorous nominating procedure. Since we wanted to talk with educators who were widely regarded as leaders, we asked six different networks[1] to nominate "educators who are changing their organizations in positive ways." Of the more than 200 nominees, nearly two dozen received nominations from more than one network. From this narrow pool, we selected 12 subjects who, as a group, represented a variety of roles,[2] types of school district, regions of the state, gender, and race. Figure 7.1 summarizes the demographic data on the subjects.

To conduct the interviews, we traveled across the state of New York, at times touching three borders: one interview was conducted on the shores of Lake Erie; another, within sight of Canada and Lake Champlain; a third, near New Jersey. We met school leaders in vibrant schools and cloistered central offices. Considering the many differences among the educators we interviewed and their diverse work settings, we did not expect this group of leaders to share the common experiences, skills, or strengths that they do. All impressed us as being skilled administrators with a positive self-image, a no-nonsense demeanor, and a propensity to action.

From an analysis of the field notes and transcripts gathered from the interviews, we drew some connections between the visions of these 12 school administrators and their work lives. Our synthesis falls into three categories: the nature of their visions, how they actualize their visions, and the relationship between leaders' visions and their careers.

The Nature of Vision

A vision is a blueprint of a desired state. It is an image of a preferred condition that we work to achieve in the future. In chapter 3, David C. Dwyer, Bruce Barnett, and Ginny Lee call vision "an overarching goal." Hickman and Silva (1984, 151) call it a "mental journey from the known to the unknown." Blumberg and Greenfield (1986, 228) relate vision to "moral imagination" that "gives that individual the ability to see that the world need not remain as it is—that it is possible for it to be otherwise—and to be better." Vision is what people work toward. One leader, a school superintendent, spoke about vision in personal terms:

---

[1] The networks were mainly New York State (NYS) organizations: the NYS Principals' Association, the NYS Superintendents' Association, the NYS ASCD chapter, professors of educational administration in NYS colleges and universities, a male and female administrator in each of the 43 NYS intermediate units who were working on a project for the NYS Education Department, and the director of a local principals' center.

[2] All subjects were school administrators; none were teachers. The need to limit the scope of the study led us to focus on one group of educators. We do not intend to imply that teachers are not educational leaders. Rather, we see the need for a parallel study conducted with teachers as subjects.

Fig. 7.1 Demographic Information on the Leaders

Subject	Position			Type of district				Region of state				Gender	Race
	Princ.	Supt.	Other	Big city	Small city	Suburb	Rural	North	West	East	Central		
1	HS					X			X			M	W
2		S				X					X	M	W
3		ASI			X						X	F	W
4	ES						X	X				F	W
5	MS					X			X			M	W
6		ASI					X	X				F	W
7	HS						X			X		M	W
8	HS					X			X			M	W
9			DDS	X						X		M	B
10		S		X							X	F	W
11		S			X					X		F	B
12		S					X			X		F	B
TOTALS	5	2 ASI / 4 S	1	2	2	4	4	2	3	4	3	6M / 6F	9 W / 3 B

Key:

HS	= High school principal		M	= Male
MS	= Middle school principal		F	= Female
ES	= Elementary school principal		W	= White
S	= Superintendent		B	= Black
ASI	= Assistant superintendent for instruction			
DDS	= Deputy district superintendent (intermediate unit)			

I believe you need to carry around dreams. You begin to see scenarios in your head. We're going to combine our two high schools some day, and I can already see the first assembly when all the kids come together. I can already see the parade through town when we celebrate it. When you're in a place long enough, you actually attend one of those scenarios [that you dreamed]. That really is exciting.

Do all leaders have a vision? After our discussions with these 12 educators, we inferred that each has a *professional mission*.[3] When we asked for confirmation that they were describing a vision or a dream of theirs, each agreed. This group of educational leaders is not unique. Bennis and Nanus (1985), who interviewed 90, "trend-directing" leaders in the corporate and public sector, also report that all their subjects "had an agenda, an unparalleled concern with outcome." Their finding, which is similar to ours, suggests that a focus on the possibilities is central to the work of leaders recognized as change agents.

Effectiveness is a key notion. Rutherford (1985), reporting on a University of Texas at Austin study, notes that, when asked, effective principals can describe their visions. He also concludes that "the less effective principals had no vision for their schools; they focused on maintaining tranquility in the here and now" (p. 32).

Although all our leaders have an image of a preferred future, a vision, none has the same vision in mind. Two categories of vision exist for our leaders: organizational and universal. Visions in the organizational category focus on the school or district where the leader works. Visions in the universal category are broader; they extend across several organizations. (See fig. 7.2.)

Organizational Vision

The first category of vision relates to *organizational excellence*. Four principals talked at length about building superb schools. One stated, "I wanted to make the kids realize that they had the best high school in the North Country." Another said, "I want every teacher in the school to be glad they're here and every other teacher in town to wish they were here."

Two others with an organizational vision are superintendents. Like the principals, their purpose is to work toward excellence, although these district

---

[3] We tried not to bias the sample. When asking for nominations, we avoided the term *vision*. Instead, we asked for the names of educators who are committed to school and schooling; who are clear about what they are trying to achieve; and who bring diverse people together to accomplish a goal, that is, their preferred future. When interviewing subjects we also avoided the term *vision*. We began by asking about the leader's goals as an educator. Only after a subject described what we thought was a vision did we verify our perception by asking, "Is your vision, then, to _____?"

Figure 7.2   Two Categories of Vision

	ORGANIZATIONAL	UNIVERSAL
Goal	Excellence in the organization	Equity for a target group
Orientation	One school or district	All schools or districts
Central concern	Creating the best	Righting a wrong

leaders focus on creating an outstanding school district. One said, "My goal is a very simple one. It's just to be sure that good teaching is going on in every classroom."

All the leaders with visions of organizational excellence seem to have a clear notion of where they are going. Somehow each, by a different path, has developed a sense of what the excellent, healthy organization is. They use this silhouette or template of the healthy school much as a physician uses an understanding of the healthy, well-functioning body. With the vision or silhouette of excellence in mind, the school leader assesses the organization and finds a discrepancy. On the basis of the diagnosis, the educator conceives a prescription to alleviate the situation.

Dwyer and the other authors of chapter 3 identify this vision as an "overarching goal." Manasse (1984) and Rutherford (1985) also describe principals with personal visions of effective, excellent schools. A recent ASCD publication by Patterson, Perkey, and Parker (1986) offers excellent suggestions about developing and actualizing an organizational vision.

Blumberg and Greenfield (1986) point out the moral component of how to apply competing standards of goodness that leaders need to address when discussing vision. They note that, "to lead a school well, one must have a vision of what is desirable and possible in that school's context" (p. 226). Reading the transcripts of the leaders with visions of excellence, we had the impression that these educators are driving or pushing their organizations toward the preferred future they have in mind.

Universal Visions

The second category of vision extends beyond the organization in which the leader works. The six whose vision fell in this category have a dual image of their preferred futures. They have the organizational excellence vision already described. They also exert considerable energy toward a second, more universal purpose which centers on an *issue of equity* that encompasses the entire educational scene. All the issue-related visions described to us concern righting a wrong.

Although the leaders with a universal vision have a passion for equity, their target groups differ. One's vision is that underprivileged children will achieve an equal education. Another's vision of equity focuses on racial integration. A third concerns an equal role for women administrators. The vision of a fourth relates to professional development. A fifth leader's vision of equity is of a community school where children and adults learn from each other. A sixth leader is deeply committed to effective-schools research.

But the same silhouette or notion of health that assists these leaders with their organizational visions does not guide their universal visions. They are dreamers as well as physicians. In several cases, their universal images of a preferred future has no template. These leaders are not following a pattern—they are making one.

The dreams of these visionaries do not impede their competence. They convinced us that they can balance their dreams and the reality of competing priorities in the schools. These leaders know how to get things done. They accomplish the many tasks that keep an organization out of trouble and on the road toward excellence. At the same time, their passion for equity spurs them to goals and actions that reach for the more perfect world they envision.

Although they are activists, the leaders with a universal vision of equity are not cultists. While each identified important significant others in their lives who also strive toward their image of a preferred future, none seems to have a group of "followers." These leaders described their relationships with like-minded individuals in collegial rather than cultish ways. But after reading their transcripts, we decided these leaders are far ahead of their subordinates and their colleagues in other schools or districts. We had the sense that these leaders are pulling all of us toward a future that we would all prefer.

Vision and Career

The careers of leaders with an organizational vision and the careers of leaders with a universal vision differed. As a group, the six leaders with universal visions hold more diverse roles. Both subgroups had principals and superintendents, but the leaders with a universal vision also included an assistant superintendent for instruction, a deputy superintendent in an intermediate unit, and the superintendent of a Special Act school district. Three of the universal-vision leaders selected their present roles so that they could enact their visions. The others said they dismiss offers of more prestigious jobs because they do not see that assuming a new role will increase their ability to enact their universal visions.

Another career decision that relates to the nature of the leaders' vision is the decision to earn a doctorate degree. Four of the six leaders with an organizational vision do not hold a doctorate, although one is in a doctoral

---

Figure 7.3   Steps Leaders Take to Actualize Their Visions

1. Valuing   They see the vision.

2. Reflection   They "own" the vision.

3. Articulation   They make their private vision a public one.

4. Planning   They develop strategies.

5. Action   They mobilize people.

---

program. On the other hand, four of the six with a universal vision do hold a doctorate; the other two are in the process of earning one. Therefore, a leader's vision relates to two career decisions: the selection of an educational role and the decision to earn a doctorate.

Actualizing the Vision

Where do leaders' visions come from? How does the presence of a vision affect leaders' work lives? We found five themes from the data that help to explain how educational leaders develop and actualize their organizational and universal visions.

In Figure 7.3, the five themes are listed, but the process is not so sequential. To a certain extent, one step provides the foundation for the next. However, all the tasks associated with one step are not necessarily accomplished before the tasks on the next step are confronted. Several of the leaders spoke about pursuing tasks on several steps concurrently. Not all the leaders have seen their visions become reality. On the contrary, all the leaders seem to be in the process of actualizing their visions. The steps of the model represent tasks they have accomplished or intend to accomplish in the pursuit of their visions.

Step 1: Valuing

For all the leaders, the emergence of their visions connects to strongly held values. As they talked about their personal and professional lives, we realized that by the time they became professional educators, their values were firmly established. We could trace the visions described to people's values, although all the leaders described their visions as emerging only after they were well into their educational careers. From their work experiences, each realized that "there was something wrong" with the way things were done. One leader, a superintendent, described the process:

It happens when you are deeply committed and it appears that outside forces constrict you. It is an irritant. Just like with an oyster, you create a pearl around the grain of irritation.

For one principal who is strongly committed to excellence in her elementary school, the essential ingredient is a helping relationship between teacher and child. She believes all school services should support that relationship. Once, when she was a teacher, she was working with a student who was having difficulty with writing.

I asked the principal for a little tape recorder. And I couldn't have it. There was no money. I know now that there was money. So whenever the teachers come to me, if there's any way that I can get it for them, I make sure that I get it for them. It's very difficult to try to do something and not have the right materials.

All the leaders shared a common value—it may be a value that all educators share—that schools should be a good places for children. One leader, a superintendent who was a high school dropout, said:

Part of me is that girl who just did not fit into that high school in Brooklyn and feels deeply that the system has to be responsive to human beings. You can't just chop them up and grind them up like so many sausages.

For 9 of the 12 leaders, an event at work led them to conclude that their school wasn't a good place for some children or that some schools aren't good places for all children. For some, this understanding led to their vision of an excellent school (or district) that would be good for all the children there. For others, a universal vision emerged, a vision that includes all schools as good places for children and adults.

Step 2: Reflection

For many of the leaders, the conclusion that "something is wrong," was closely followed by the thought "I can do something about it." In Step 2, reflection on this thought led to a personal dedication to the vision.

In our estimation, three of the leaders have an organizational vision and are working to commit themselves to a universal vision. Their path is still unclear to them, but they see that someone must do something to alleviate the situation that concerns them. These leaders are certain that a problem exists, but they are uncertain that they can provide the solution. They believe in themselves. Each has received positive reinforcement about their leadership from several significant others: superiors, mentors, family members, or colleagues.

However, they all realize that to "make a difference" they will need to invest themselves and to take professional risks. While they want to make a difference, they are reflecting about whether they are willing to pay the price.

They fear that in "owning" the vision, it will "own" them.

Part of this fear lies in a perception that a personal dedication to their vision will negatively affect their family life. For those who are planning a family or whose children are young, this decision is an especially difficult one. Those with established families have negotiated an agreement with their spouses about their careers.

Step 3: Articulation

If a leader's reflection leads to a commitment to a vision, the next step is sharing the vision with others. This process involves speaking from a position of high visibility and developing a public image.

Five of the twelve leaders talked at length about career decisions they made to gain a visible position. All the leaders recognize that they need to assume a formal leadership role in education to make an impact. Some were administrators when the vision emerged, so (especially if their vision was an organizational one) they already had the formal authority to begin to enact the vision by sharing it with others. Others search for the "right" place. One leader stated, "I applied and interviewed in several districts, but it took time to find the glove that was a good fit." Articulating a vision seems to require an appropriate speaking platform, one where the leader can expect to influence others.

Even after they have achieved a high-visibility position, leaders with both organizational and universal visions work to develop their professional image outside the organization. One aspect of image building is "getting good press"; therefore, leaders learn so they can share the vision with a wider audience. Another aspect of image building involves assuming leadership roles in professional associations. Thus, leaders can touch colleagues in other school districts and share the vision with them.

Step 4: Planning

Many of these leaders are strategists. A vision, by its nature, is a target. But the plans these leaders make to reach their distant targets are not a sequential series of steps that, if taken in turn, will lead to the target. Rather, they are a series of contingency plans. With the distant target in mind, the leader develops a series of "plays," much as a football team develops a game plan. Then, as each play occurs, the leader reassesses and, if necessary, adjusts the game plan. These leaders value planning, and they are proud when their plans succeed. One leader said:

A crude way of putting it is: when I was a kid growing up, Willie Mays was a really fine center fielder. I remember my Dad used to say: "You notice Willie Mays never has to make a fancy catch. He always catches the ball right in front of him—easily." I have that notion about organizations. We should never look like we are making a fancy catch here. It should always look very easy. I feel that if I am doing my job, I'm thinking four or five years ahead. What's going on today, this year, should be going on easily because of the stuff we put in place.

This habit of formulating strategies develops as leaders become more experienced. They learn that things rarely proceed as planned, so they need to keep an "ear to the ground." Several of the leaders named key people who are their regular sources of information. They also emphasized the importance of understanding the system, of being able to determine how it works and how people function in it. They asserted that, without this baseline knowledge, good planning cannot occur.

Finally, the leaders who have most successfully enacted their visions seem to be masters at identifying resources. They are aware of unconventional sources of funds. They develop creative strategies to secure new funds from conventional sources. What might be an obstacle to others becomes a sweet challenge to these leaders.

Step 5: Action

Without action, visions and the plans to enact them are useless. The leaders are, above all, doers. The lists of their accomplishments are long. Our nomination process ensured that the identified leaders enjoy a wide reputation among educators as people who get things done.

Their ability to act seems to relate to their competence as administrators and their well-developed people and political skills. They all realize that people are central to their vision. During the interviews, we observed how smoothly they all related to us, and we asked about their working relationships with others. We concluded that these leaders are strong, skillful communicators, although they project different demeanors. Some have cool relationships with subordinates; others have warm ones.

Most describe themselves as demanding. They are unwilling to cover for people in the organization who block their vision. All expressed a willingness to work with a subordinate who lacks a skill, but all stressed their intolerance of mediocrity and complacency. One principal said:

You fix it so that people either will work with you or leave. I had some people on the faculty who said to me, "I don't like this. I don't think it is going to work. It is only going to make things worse." I encourage them to seek transfers.

Our visionary leaders work well with diverse people. They also search for and reward strong, able colleagues. Rather than being threatened by other's abilities, they purposely search for them:

I want administrators around me who are smarter than I am. They cause me to think differently. They can see the big picture. They can see beyond the daily structure of administrative problems. When I make a snap decision, they say, "Wait a minute. If you

102

do that, then this will happen. And then, as a result, something else may happen. So you've got to think about that again."

The Impact of Vision

As a group, these leaders are clearly special people. They are interesting. They feel productive. They convey a feeling of worth. They are not burned out; they are fired up.

However, having a vision does not make life easy. The leaders described long hours at work, often in conflict situations. They invest time, energy, and money in perfecting the skills they need to accomplish their vision. They take on taxing jobs. They have problems negotiating a balance between family and professional responsibilities.

These leaders take risks. Holders of an organizational vision talk about taking an unpopular, even courageous, stand in their organization. They confronted the faculty, the parents, the superintendent, the Board of Education, and the community. Holders of a universal vision dare to propose a different way of approaching education.

These leaders seize opportunities. Taking and making opportunities is an important aspect of their work lives. A superintendent described his guiding principle:

I read a marvelous little book called *Plunkett of Tammany Hall* in a theory of government course at Harvard. Plunkett was a minor operative in Tammany Hall who did very well. Someone asked him what his secret was. He said, "Well, I seen my opportunities and I took 'em." I think if you are looking ahead and you bump into the opportunities—whether it is a community ready to move or a staff that has some good ideas—you put them in a special culture. You try to grow them up a little bit.

Finally, having a sense of vision provides leaders with a purpose (Manasse 1984), but it also presents them with a struggle. As one leader said: "I have to decide whether it drives me or I drive it. I make my best decision when I am driving. Otherwise, I'm consumed. It's an internal struggle, but it's worth it because I really want to make a difference."

References

Bennis, Warren, and Burt Nanus. *Leaders: The Strategies for Taking Charge*. New York: Harper & Row, 1985.

Blumberg, Arthur, and William Greenfield. *The Effective Principal: Perspectives on School Leadership*. Boston: Allyn and Bacon, 1980.

Blumberg, Arthur, and William Greenfield. *The Effective Principal: Perspectives on School Leadership*, 2nd ed. Boston: Allyn and Bacon, 1986.

Hickman, Craig R., and Michael A. Silva. *Creating Excellence: Managing Corporate Culture, Strategy, and Change in the New Age*. New York: New American Library, 1984.

Manasse, A. Lorri. "Principals as Leaders of High Performing Systems." *Educational Leadership*, 41, 5 (February 1984) 42–46.

Patterson, Jerry L., Stuart C. Purkey, and Jackson V. Parker. *Productive School Systems for a Nonrational World*. Alexandria, Va: ASCD, 1986.

Peters, Thomas J., and Robert H. Waterman. *In Search of Excellence*. New York: Harper & Row, 1982.

Rutherford, William L., Shirley M. Hord, Leslie L. Huling, and Gene E. Hall. *Change Facilitators: In Search of Understanding Their Role*. Report #3159. Washington, D.C.: National Institute of Education, 1983.

8

The Conscience of Leadership

Thomas F. Green

M aking ethical sense of professional practice requires a grasp of the point of the profession. If we can clearly see the point of our profession, then the ethical sense of day-to-day practice will become more evident.

It follows from this fact that the term "professional ethics" is a redundancy. The first part of this chapter is intended to explain why that is so, and the second part aims to explore the many ways that the point of the professional enterprise shapes our conscience—that is to say, our capacity to criticize our own practice and that of others.

The Redundancy of "Professional Ethics"

In the past 20 years or so, I have been privileged to work with a good many persons in what seem to me rather lofty executive positions in government, universities, and business. And I have noted that among these acquaintances, there are some whose sense of courtesy apparently demands that if they arrive at a meeting late, they should make up for the offense by leaving early. Being persons of both courtesy and justice, they apparently aspire to make the remedy proportional to the offense. The result is that the later they arrive, the earlier they apparently feel impelled to leave. Adhering to this rule of justice, they should end by leaving before they come or, in short, by not coming at all.

Now, I believe that we should be indulgent, even charitable, toward these people. Typically, they are busy, torn in their loyalties, and faced with difficulties in managing their time. Often, they have to spend hours and days on matters that they would prefer to leave alone. They have to pretend to attend carefully to many proposed alternatives for action, even when they know that only a few exist.

But what is it that leads to this peculiar moral chemistry by which virtue turns into vice and care is changed to neglect? I suggest it is a problem that we all face; only we do not see it nearly as clearly in our own case as we do in persons of high position. I do not mean to complain about such behavior. This way of acting, for all I know, may be a necessary consequence of executive position. It may be a consequence, but it cannot be the point. This chemistry, turning gold into lead, stems, I suggest, from a simple failure to keep "the point" in view.

In the early books of Plato's *Republic*, Socrates urges a similar argument on Thrasymachus. Thrasymachus argues that justice is simply whatever is in the interest of the stronger. He apparently believes that because rulers have power that they can (and possibly do) use to advance their own interests, therefore, advancing their own interests must be the essential point of ruling. But Socrates describes this definiton as the confusion of two arts. In counterargument, he points to the case of physicians who, even today, may confuse the arts of healing and the arts of gain and, by such perversion, fail to see the point of their practice.

These are different versions of the fallacy of displacement or the forgotten point. We indulge it in a thousand ways. We discern, for example, what is undoubtedly true, namely that friends are useful to us. But then we are inclined to go ahead and suppose what is erroneous, namely that we need friends because they are useful, and so using them becomes the point of friendship. But surely utility is not the point: Use your friends and you will have none; pick your friends for their utility and you will lose whatever friends you have. In like manner, being educated is useful, but education's utility is not its point.

Suppose we teach young journalists how to market their skills, how to sell their work to magazines and other publishers, but teach them nothing about the history of the printed page, the function of communication, or the fragile nature of the institutions of free speech. Suppose we teach them about libel laws and how to stay within them, but not why they matter. Then, we teach them the skill, but not the point of the skill. Suppose we teach students of public administration the problems of budgeting and planning, but not that budgeting is the principal means of making values concrete and distributing such goods as security and health and recreation. In short, suppose again we teach them the skill, but not the point. Suppose we teach teachers that no subject is more valuable than any other, that they must attend to "the cognitive" as well as "the affective" (as though the two were ever separated except in totally trivial matters). What counts, we say to young teachers, is learning to learn, not coming to know, and knowing one thing is no more important than knowing another. Again, we teach the skills of teaching, but not the point.

These suppositions typify the paradigm of bad education—the kind that converts literature into a technical craft, public service into management, and education into manipulation. This education is socially disastrous because it is not *educationally* serious. This education has no educational point. As my former colleague, Paul Dietl, once wrote in an unpublished essay: "If all we get are students who perform according to rules, students who do not see the point of what they are doing, then we will not have all we want anymore than we will if we get students who are civil to one another but do not see the good of it all—no love, no anger, no pride, no shame."[1] For example, providing special courses in ethics for engineers reflects our failure to teach engineering, not our failure to teach ethics. We teach them to possess the technique, but not how to become possessed by the point of the practice. Again, we can discern the fallacy of displacement.

To the extent that we have moral or ethical problems in one of the professions we do not know what the profession is *about*. For example, many of the discussed problems of "medical ethics" arise from the fact that the purpose of medicine is no longer clear in our minds. We do not know whether its aim is the preservation or restoration of health or whether it is simply the avoidance of death. We have the technical capacity to keep people alive even after anything resembling the status of "person" has vanished from the life we preserve. This technical capability seems to present ethical problems. But the problems arise partly because we are no longer clear whether the practice of medicine is aimed at the preservation of life or at the prevention of death or when the one aim becomes transformed into the other. Thus, we tend to see a problem. But is it a medical problem? Is it a problem of medical practice or medical ethics or does it represent instead a crisis in our consciousness of the point of medical practice itself?

It is quite likely that we will translate the problem into a question of liability instead of the practice of medicine. We translate it into a legal problem of determining who can be held accountable for an act that might end a life, forgetting along the way that death, besides being the end of life, is also a natural part of life. We tend, also, to frame the issues in the language of rights rather than in the language of harm and thus seek to preserve the rights of all involved and neglect the harm we may be doing along the way. Instead of clarifying the point of medical practice, we turn in other directions, which may well cause the problems to appear as issues of professional ethics.

But one should attend to the very phrase "professional ethics." Some have described it as an oxymoron, an evident contradiction, like "transparently covert action," or "cooperative competition." If "professional" ethics exists, does "non-professional" ethics? If "applied" ethics exists, does "unapplied" ethics? What in our culture, in our understanding of ethics, stands in the way of our *hearing* the monumental redundancy in the phrase? Our deafness stems from our commitment to the fallacy of displacement—our simple failure to see the point.

---

[1] Personal correspondence.

Right now, professional ethics is a growth industry in the academic world. For many, mostly those in the humanities, it often seems the only expanding business in town. Yet why do we fail to see that by the very term "profession" we refer already to a kind of practice that is not merely incidentally, but essentially, a moral enterprise? In their social organization, professions are associations with a collegial structure—they are governed by their members. But what kinds of norms do their members use to govern? Professions are also typically gatherings of experts. Strong norms of moral force cannot, however, emerge within the collegial order from "the knowledge base." The technical norms of a practice can at best produce a kind of technical competence, the sort of competence that I have already referred to as knowing the skill, but not the point.

If they are to be moral associations, then their norms must be derived from a third feature of professions, namely that they are always practiced in response to some fundamental human need or social good whose advancement is already a moral aim. Medicine, nursing, law, and the priesthood constitute the paradigmatic professions. They answer to the basic needs for a human response to pain and pathology, to the search for health, to the need for justice and the maintenance of social order, and for meaning at the major events of life—birth, death, and all the joinings and partings of human beings. The professions, in short, are practices related to the central life-giving, life-sustaining, and life-fulfilling events of human existence. The need for them is bounded only by natality, plurality, and death. Thus, we can speak easily of these as professions and cannot speak so easily of hula-hooping and "making book" in the same way. These latter may be ways of making a living, and so, in a loose way of speaking, they may even produce careers. But no one with even a shred of historical consciousness could speak of them as callings or even vocations.

Thus, if we seek to induct persons into a profession by giving them command of the relevant expertise, and if at the same time we neglect to teach them the point of the practice, then surely we will need to offer instruction in professional ethics. But that need will arise from our failure to teach the point of the profession, not from our failure to teach ethics. Since the problem does not arise from our failure to teach ethics, it will not go away because of our success in teaching ethics.

Rather than teaching ethcis, we must teach the point of profession. Seeing the point is the first step in grasping the ethics of any profession, and thus it is a first step in grasping the ethics of educational leadership. It may be the last step as well. But in any case, we need to see that the ethics of professions derive first from the mere fact that they are professions in this sense. Ethics is an integral part of the profession, not something added.

The moral character of the profession does not derive from its body of technical expertise. It derives rather from the fact that a profession is a social practice that is already moral. Physicians had moral and social authority long before they had much of anything in the way of a science or technical expertise.

What, then, can be regarded as the professional practice of educational leadership? The practice of educational leadership is aimed at education in the same way that medical practice is aimed at health. But the need for education is more ubiquitous. I need a physician when I am suffering from some pathology, a lawyer when things are disrupted. But when do I need a teacher? When I am ignorant? Is there a time when I am not ignorant about something? What condition does educational leadership aim at? Is it wisdom? That is too much. Economic independence and citizenship? These are too minimal. The answer is simply not clear. But its lack of clarity should not dissuade us.

If we cannot discover an answer to this question, then perhaps we will have to conclude that educational leadership is not a professional activity at all. But whatever the answer, it clearly cannot be simply the successful and efficient management of the educational enterprise. If educational leadership is a profession, it can be defined by its response to some central human need, which will then provide the ethics of the practice. However we argue the case, again and again we will come back to the simple claim that educational leadership answers to the human need for the practice of education. In short, the professional aim is to educate.

This claim may seem too obvious even to need any discussion. Still, the purpose is often forgotten. Educational excellence is seldom on the public agenda for education. Instead, we hear that the aim of educational leadership must be to restore American dominance in world markets, or to preserve the national security, or to assist in the maintenance of domestic peace and tranquility, or to provide a basis for each person to successfully negotiate the problems of attaining economic self-sufficiency in the labor market.

Of course, successful management of the educational enterprise at all levels will secure these goods. But to confuse these consequences with the aim of educational leadership is to confuse the point with the consequences of attending to the point. It would be like confusing the need for friends with the consequences of having friends. It would be to commit the fallacy of displacement.

What is it to educate? How does educational worth relate to aggregate social worth or individual utility? Although these are perhaps the most unasked questions on the educational scene, they are not the most un-answered questions. They are answered willy-nilly all the time, but the answers are unreflective. Asking these questions and getting clear about them is the most direct path toward getting clear about the ethics of educational leadership. Educational leaders may have moral problems in their practice, not because they are unethical or because they lack a sense of honor, but because they lack a clear understanding, a clear vision, of what their practice is centrally about, namely what it means to educate. The ethics of education will be derived from a clear image of its practice.

The Limits of Conscience

By conscience I mean simply the many ways we have to be critical of ourselves and others in the performance of our life tasks. The conscience of a professional, then, refers to the ways we have of criticizing our own and others' professional conduct. I speak of these as "voices" to reflect the fact that they seem to be present in all ages and more or less consciously in all persons. (I do not take a developmental view of the matter.) We can discern the voices of craft, membership, duty, memory, and imagination.

Thus, the problems of ethics can be construed as arising from the conversation between these different voices. If there were no conflict between these different voices, there would be no ethical problems of leadership. There would be only the problem of management. If there were no differences in what these voices commanded, then there would be no problems of ethics. We would know the answers to our dilemmas, and the only problem would be to comply.

Craft

Many aspects of educational leadership are simply matters of craft or skill. We are likely to describe these as merely technical affairs. The central ethics of leadership is not derived from technical skill, but leadership cannot be exercised without it. Ineptness is a fault in educational leaders just as it is in wives and husbands. In fact, the image of the moral life as a life of skill is very old. It was the central metaphor in the ancient Greek construct of the matter. This image led to the idea that knowledge is virtue. If one knows how to live, then one is more likely to live well. Only in the modern world do we think excellence in such practical matters as planning, motivating, and managing budgets are not moral demands. We tend to recognize that such skills are needed but to respond, at the same time, by claiming that their possession is not a moral matter.

As one of my correspondents said, "I know people who are inept, but they are not immoral." The inference is that being unskillful is not a moral matter. The "bad" in "doing badly" is not a moral "bad"; it has nothing to do with ethics. My correspondent, of course, reflects the modern view of ethics and moral education. These matters of skill are not usually viewed as moral concerns. But it is precisely that modern view of the boundaries of the moral that I want to suggest is mistaken. That is the modern view that, I suggest, does not serve us well and that we need to eschew.

The mistake has two consequences. First, it inclines us to accept the view that because mere technical skill is not necessarily a moral demand we can either ignore it and say it doesn't matter, or say that management is the only thing that matters in leadership and it has nothing to do with ethics. Thus, we set up a dangerous contrast between what we mean by being prudentially skillful and being moral. How many times have we heard someone say that educational leadership is not a matter of ethics; it is mostly politics? This attitude is meant to convey the conviction that ethics does not have much to do with being skillful, with being good at what we do. This view is a mistake. Lack of skill is a fault, and it is a fault of conscience in anyone for whom such a fault stirs no sense of failure. In contrast, the conscience of craft is present and evident whenever people practicing the profession are dissatisfied with slovenly, inept work and are driven to reject it even when it occurs in themselves. A conscience would allow no other judgment.

But this division between morality and prudence has another consequence. It allows us to suppose that ethical or moral matters arise only when we are confronted with dilemmas. As Pincoffs[2] said, such a view of ethics cultivates the thought that we are not engaged in moral matters except when we are in a moral quandary. This disposition leads people to suppose that we do not teach the ethics of leadership except when we pose ultimate or nearly ultimate choices—the so-called lifeboat-type of problem. But such matters as getting things done on time, doing them well, and exercising foresight are matters of ethics, and they should and do weigh on the professional conscience whenever professionals dare to consult the reach of their sense of competence and its importance.

Membership

The conscience of membership is sometimes classed under the heading of *loyalty*, which is partly what it is. But only a part. Educational leadership is always carried on within some community of which the leader is a member. In fact, it is always carried out among many communities and in the midst of many memberships, some momentary, some more durable, and some extending over an entire lifetime. We live, for example, as members of a professional guild, as citizens at various levels of aggregation, as family members or church members, and as members of many local and more limited communities, sometimes of an ethnic or racial stripe. Memberships are attachments, and attachments are forged by ties of social norms. Membership, in short, always carries with it certain limits of behavior, and those limits impose constraints on conscience. They define some judgments of right and wrong, or good and bad.

---

[2] E. Pincoffs, "Quandary Ethics," in *Revisions, Changing Perspectives in Moral Philosophy,* by S. Houerwas and A. MacIntyre (West Bend, Ind.: Notre Dame Press, 1983).

Social norms are not simply rules describing the statistically modal behavior in a social group. Rather, they are rules prescribing what persons in that social group should do. The test that a particular norm exists is not whether members comply with the rule but whether they adopt a critical view of behavior that departs from the rule. Thus, social norms are important because they describe what behavior members will critically appraise and perhaps condemn even in themselves. In short, a social norm is a rule of conscience. But it is not a rule merely for the individual. Norms are rules for individuals as members. The formation of conscience, even conscience itself, is never in this respect a purely private matter. On the contrary, insofar as we can speak of the conscience of membership, conscience is always a strictly public affair. Although our conscience is uniquely our own and no one else's and, therefore, in a sense private, nevertheless it is doubtful that conscience can ever be formed except within some public, some membership, and for the sake of life within that public.

These observations are important for the ethics of educational leadership because the educational leader is simultaneously engaged in shaping the social norms of several memberships. Educating, not something else, is the task of educational leadership. Social norms educate. They educate, they form, the conscience of membership. Indeed, they constitute the conscience of membership. So the educational leader needs to find a balance among the various memberships that compete for attention and impose sometimes conflicting duties. The educational leader also needs to be skillful in the actual creation of social norms in the school or college, altering, for example, the description of students from "those present" to those who are "members." Shaping the norms and making them public is a central task of educational leaders. One can hardly imagine a leader who does not keep this clear aim in mind.

Sacrifice

The clearest, most self-evident moral voice is the voice of sacrifice. We hear this voice when self-interest and duty conflict. Indeed, the gravity of the commands of duty is clearest in the presence of a conflict with our own self-interest. We know that in these situations, the demands of duty should prevail. This is the voice of morality that my correspondent referred to when he said he knew of people who were inept but not for that reason immoral. It is not that they are insensitive to the needs of their neighbors, just that they are inept in pursuing those needs. That ineptness is not immoral. Although the voice of duty is not all there is to conscience, this voice of conscience as sacrifice is the voice most typically viewed as the voice of morality.

Indeed, when duty and self-interest conflict, we all know how the voice of duty struggles to be heard, let alone followed. Our desire is to quiet it. In short, between the two, self-interest seems the strongest and most natural to acknowledge. But the voice of duty is stern. For example, one of our elected chief state school officers wanted to provide better educational resources for children in his state than would have been provided without him. He cultivated an understanding with his evaluation staff that they were to find the best information on the condition of the schools and to report it accurately and clearly to the people of the state—favorable or not. To this instruction he added a single proviso—no surprises, no revelations, within three months of an election. And to this proviso he added a single sanction: If he discovered that they did not follow these directions—if he found inadequate or concealed data, for example—then he would ask for their jobs within 36 hours.

Now, I do not know, but I suspect, that he got a greater degree of skill and competence from his staff and more candor with the public than he would have if he had assumed a more calculated posture resting on an appeal to the moral impulses of his staff. He clearly appealed to their self- interest, not to their sense of duty. He did not risk the possibility that they would still the voice of duty in favor of the voice of self-interest.

This school official's story reminds us of the view that self-interest exercises a stronger tug, on the whole, than morality. Self-interested behavior is often not the same as moral behavior, and the two from time to time may conflict. Nevertheless, he reminds us that we can get a greater degree of honest behavior by appealing to that self-interest than we might by appealing to people's good moral character. We can get moral behavior (not morality) by addressing the prudential side of the conflict between interest and duty. This story illustrates, then, the kind of halfway house between the voice of duty and the tug of self-interest. The halfway house appropriately acknowledges the voice of sacrifice but at the same time realistically appraises its weakness. Still, we should not denigrate the educational value of the halfway house. It may not produce the strongest moral conscience, but it points in the right direction. It is a useful formative direction, a place where we can rest while we wait for the transformation of human beings into saints.

But consider a case where the voice of sacrifice is not simply sought, but must be displayed. There can hardly be anything more contrary to self-interest than being fired. Yet, for anyone in a position of public educational leadership, sooner or later (probably sooner than later) one will be invited to resign. It simply goes with the territory. It may come with the next election, or the next school board, or the next change in vital legislation. Suppose we ask, "Under what conditions would one find it acceptable to resign?" The answer will reveal a great deal. Ask it of yourself and you will begin to discover in the structure of your own conscience the points at which the voice of duty will surmount the tug of self-interest.

The suggestion, of course, is that since I will be asked to resign, part of the exercise of excellence in leadership is to act to ensure that the request for resignation comes over something that matters. In short, I should act so that the voice of duty can prevail and does not clash with self-interest. But we can press the matter another step. Suppose we ask, "Under what conditions would I refuse to resign and insist on being fired?" Properly calculated, this latter act can be made to occur over a point of undoubted duty. In that event, there will be a temporary reversal of authority. I have the chance for a press conference and the opportunity to make a public, perhaps even a moral, point—a temporary reversal to be sure. But it does provide an opportunity, even an opportunity for educational leadership. Under what conditions would I seek it? These are some of the boundary questions of conscience. When we ask them of ourselves, we begin to see how our own conscience is put together, and we can better decide whether what we find is worthy of admiration.

Imagination and Memory

Social memory, moral imagination, and their interdependence are essential voices of conscience, especially among leaders, because we cannot do without rootedness and criticism, without tradition and dissatisfaction with tradition. No one can stand apart to criticize the existing order of things without standing somewhere. No leader can lead without a vision of how things might be in the light of how things are and have been. The idea that educating begins with a *tabula rasa* may be a helpful, even a plausible, fiction, but the notion that communities of membership started today or just yesterday has not a shred of plausibility. Communities are all rooted in history, even revolutionary communities. But even without the history, every educational leader must be rooted in some kind of historical membership.

Think of the Old Testament prophets. Theirs was the voice of criticism that came always from within a community already shaped by the Torah. The voice of a conscience always speaks as a community member, with all the accents, verbs, and metaphors that such membership implies. It is not and could not be an alien voice. Though those verbalizing their conscience often speak against the lived life of the community, they still speak always from within it. There is a lesson here for educational leaders. When the "professional" educator speaks in accents too technical, too far from the interior life of the community, then there is trouble. The root of the trouble is that the educator is perceived as an outsider.

There is, then, the conscience of membership but also the conscience of critical imagination. Only imagination allows us to speak to other members about the chasm that exists between the hopes and fair expectations of the community and the failures of our lived lives. In fact, the rootedness of that voice in membership gives the judgment its sting. That judgment hurts because it comes to us as the voice of an insider, speaking out of a shared memory and turning it against us to reveal how great the distance is between the ideal we espouse and the realities that we seem always to lapse into. It is not a pleasant thing to be brought to see how blind and to hear how deaf we can be.

But besides this rootedness in membership and history and that critical tone of moral imagination, this voice of conscience has another side. Whenever the voice of conscience as imagination is exercised, we are threatened. But we are also instructed and invited, pulled and drawn, into fresh beginnings. The visions of leaders are always framed in the future tense because they always portray some definite possibility that regrettably (or fortunately) is not yet but is to be in some indefinite future. But their being in the future tense, though true, is not the point. The point is rather that having given us a vision, a glimpse of an alternative context for living and acting with its own resources, its own risks, its own advantages, they invite our entrance into that future now. Leaders without vision, without rootedness, and without imagination are dangerous or at best inept. Where would they lead us? Nowhere. Nowhere at least that anyone should want to go.

This sketch of the voices of conscience is not all there is to the ethics of educational leadership. But it should provide a direction for thought, a means of keeping the point in view, a way of knowing where we are going and how to thread a path through the distractions and confusions that inevitably will intrude on the office of leadership.

9

The Theoretical Basis for Cultural Leadership

Thomas J. Sergiovanni

This yearbook is both a testimonial and a celebration. Compared with writings on school leadership as recently as a decade ago, the chapters in this yearbook attest to the significant changes taking place in how we view, understand, and practice school leadership. At the heart of these changes is the view that the meaning of leadership behavior and events to teachers and others is more important than the behavior and events themselves. Leadership reality for all groups is the reality they create for themselves, and thus leadership cannot exist separate from what people find significant and meaningful.

The idea of socially constructed reality seems distant at first. But on second thought, it is an ordinary concept. We are constantly involved in making sense of our experiences. Sense-making requires that we interpret experiences in the light of our various frames of reference. Different frames lead to different interpretations and constructions of reality. This process of sense-making is influenced by our interactions with others—a point important to the concept of school culture.

The philosopher and political scientist Charles Taylor (1981) distinguishes between brute and sense data to illustrate the importance of socially constructed reality. Brute data are the events of leadership life in raw form, objectively described and carefully documented. Sense data, on the other hand, stem from what events mean to people, how people are touched by the events, and the significance people attach to events. The organizational theorist Louis Pondy (1978) makes a similar metaphorical distinction by referring to the phonetics and semantics of leadership. Understood phonetically, leadership is concerned with people's behavior or style in the form of a descriptive rendering of their actions. Phonetic leadership is readily observed and amiable to scientific measuring in reproducible ways. The semantic side of leadership refers to its deep structure and the meanings that people attribute to and derive from the behavior and events at hand.

The old view of leadership, which emphasized style and behavior and the development of highly structured management systems, remains important. But now what leaders stand for and believe in, and their ability to communicate these values and ideals in a way that provides both meaning and significance to others, is more important than how they behave. This view, I believe, is the message of the chapters of this book, and the message revealed by countless studies of leadership in highly successful schools (e.g., Lightfoot 1983, Lipsitz 1983, Dwyer et al. 1984) and other enterprises (e.g., Peters and Waterman 1982, Deal and Kennedy 1982, Bennis and Nanus 1985, McGregor Burns, 1978, Vaill 1984).

To describe and document the forms this new leadership takes in practice and to come to grips with its concepts, values, and underlying inner structure is important. This account is in a sense a celebration of the human spirit and an acknowledgment of the importance of this spirit in determining the success of any enterprise.

Differing Theoretical Mindscapes

Many of the new insights into what leadership is, the forms it can take, and its impact on effectiveness emerge from studies of leaders and leadership in highly successful enterprises in both the public and private sector. These studies reveal that highly successful leaders view how their schools operate and what is important to teachers at work differently from ordinary leaders. The values they bring to their work and the assumptions they make about teachers at work also differ.

Although philosophers speak of world views and the consequences of different world views on a person's reality and subsequent actions, and scientists similarly speak of paradigms, I choose the more modest metaphor *mindscape* to describe this phenomenon and its effects on.practice. A mindscape is composed of a person's mental image, view, theory, and set of beliefs that orient that person to problems, help to sort out the important from the unimportant, and provide a rationale for guiding actions and decisions. A leader's mindscape helps to construct her reality. Different realities result in different decisions and different behavior; thus, the practices of highly successful leaders and their ordinary counterparts also differ.

Ordinary leaders view schools as a tightly structured form and a pattern of operation that resemble the mechanical workings of a clock. These leaders are, in a sense, captured by a clock mechanism image of cogs, gears, wheels, drives, and pins, all tightly connected in an orderly and predictable manner.

This clockworks mindscape of how schools operate is captivating and popular. Most of us like orderly things and feel comfortable with predictability and regularity in our lives. Further, this tidy and orderly clockworks mindscape simplifies the task of school management. A leader need only control and regulate the master wheel and pin, and all the other wheels and pins will move responsively and in concert. The clockworks mindscape imbues management with a sense of power and control, which in part accounts for its attractiveness.

Principals, school superintendents, state policymakers, and commissioners of education who share this mindscape of how schools and school systems work believe that they can achieve their goals by closely linking together various parts of the system and by providing the necessary management controls to ensure that the linking works properly. Thus, the process of ensuring quality schooling becomes a simple matter of detailing the goals, tightly linking these goals to the curriculum, aligning the curriculum to teaching, and teaching to testing. A management-oriented supervisory and evaluation system is typically added to allow for proper monitoring of the tightly aligned system. The system itself represents the main gears and pins of the clockworks that are to be properly established and monitored to ensure that all the other gears and pins (teachers and students) operate reliably and predictably. I refer to this clockworks view as the *Clockworks I mindscape* (Sergiovanni 1987).

Weick (1982) points out that, for the management principles associated with Clockworks I to work, the leader must assume the existence of four organizational properties: the presence of a self-correcting rational system among closely linked and interdependent people, a consensus on goals and means, their coordination by dissemination of information, and the predictability of problems and problem responses. Schools, by contrast, are considered loosely structured, with ambiguous goals and large spans of control. Weick notes that when these management principles are applied to schools, "effectiveness declines, people become confused, and work doesn't get done." In his words, the enterprises are "managed with the wrong model in mind" (p. 673). Unfortunately, this confusion is the fate of school policymakers and leaders who share in the Clockworks I mindscape—a model that does not reflect the realities of practice, that provides a limited and unsophisticated view of the nature of teaching and learning and a regressive view of the role of the teacher.

Successful leaders in both schools and the private sector view organizations differently; they have a *Clockworks II mindscape* (Sergiovanni 1987); when they open the clock, they see a mechanism gone awry. The wheels and pins are not connected but instead turn and swing independently of each other. These leaders recognize that, in the real world of organizational functioning, enterprises operate far more loosely than we commonly assume and certainly more loosely than the organizational chart depicts and more loosely than we are willing to admit (Roethlisberger and Dickson 1939, Cohen et al. 1972, Katz 1964, Bidwell 1965, Lipsky 1980, Weick 1976, March 1984).

Because of these loose connections, and despite the efforts of management, most enterprises are characterized by a great deal of de facto autonomy for workers. Loose connectedness and de facto autonomy are well-documented characteristics of schools (Sarason 1971, Lieberman and Miller 1984, Lortie 1975, Morris et al. 1984). Waller (1967) and Bidwell (1965) commented early on the structural looseness of schools. But we need not rely on experts to tell us what is so obvious from our own experience. Even a casual observer of schools sees that teachers work in isolation and interact infrequently. Further, the curriculum that matters is the one that reaches students, and that curriculum is in the minds and hearts of teachers; the tall trash can next to the teachers' mailboxes attests to unread memorandums. For all intents and purposes, a school of thirty classes is more like thirty schools than one school.

Worker and Professional Mindscapes

Mindscapes serve the dual purpose of security blanket and mind programmer. As security blankets, they help us to make sense of an uncertain world by tying life's events to the mind's logic. As mind programmers, they serve as walls that limit our vision and program the way we think about life's events. Each of the clockworks mindscapes of organizational functioning, for example, program for us how we think about other issues, such as the nature of teaching and the role of the teacher.

The Clockworks I mindscape frames teaching and learning in a fashion that is consistent with its emphasis on tight alignment and explicit structure. Teaching is conceived as a job, and the teacher is a worker. Clockworks II, on the other hand, frames teaching and teachers more in the direction of a vocation engaged in by professionals. This distinction is important because, although professionals and workers both function within the context of a work system (established principles, guidelines, knowledge bases, research findings, best practice models, standards, etc.), their relationship to this work system differs.

Workers view the system as a bureaucratic harness designed to program what is to be done, when, and how. Management labors hard to refine the system and monitor its use to ensure that workers are doing what they are supposed to and that work outputs measure up to highly specific, predetermined standards. Within the worker mindscape of teaching and teacher, teachers are invariably subordinate to the system, and in the ideal the best teaching is "teacherproof." Administrators and supervisors are expected to closely monitor this work system to ensure that its protocols are evident in the work of teachers. As monitors, administrators and supervisors exercise little independent judgment and few prerogatives. They, too, are programmed by the systems.

Professionals, by contrast, are superordinate to the work system. Instead of the work system using them, they use the work system. The work of professionals emerges from an interaction between their knowledge and individual client needs. We assume that professionals command a body of knowledge that enables them to make informed judgments in response to unique situations and individual client needs. The concept of professionalism and professional work requires sufficient degrees of freedom. Guidelines, established principles, knowledge bases, research findings, and best practice models are all important. But they do not exist to program the decisions that professionals make or to program their behavior. Instead, these tools exist to inform professionals' judgment so that their decisions are more reasoned and their behavior is more effective.

Administrators and supervisors do not view loose connectedness and de facto autonomy as organizational defects to be corrected by stronger management controls but as natural and even desirable characteristics that enhance professionals' discretionary prerogatives and free them to make relevant, informed decisions. The Clockworks II mindscape of organizational functioning and the professional mindscape of teaching are, therefore, compatible and reinforce each other.

Although highly successful and ordinary leaders do not share the same mindscapes of how schools function or about teachers and teaching, they do share a common commitment to achieving identifiable goals. Further, the leaders believe that the work of various school professionals must be coordinated if these goals are to be served well. Despite these commonalities, they follow different paths as they coordinate the work. Clockworks II leaders, for example, rely far less on traditional management controls and other bureaucratic linkages to bring about coordination. Instead, they emphasize cultural dimensions that function as "bonds" (Etzioni 1961, Schein 1985, Sergiovanni 1984, Firestone and Wilson 1985, Peters and Austin 1985) to provide the necessary connections.

The task of the leader, in their view, is not so much to link together parts of the system to link together people and events through management designs, as it is to bond people together by developing a shared covenant and common culture. The concept of organizational patriotism (Sergiovanni and Carver 1980) is important to Clockworks II leaders as they work to build commitment and loyalty to the work of the school. In the language of Etzioni's (1961) compliance theory, they seek coordination, order, and compliance in a loosely connected world, by relying on normative power and moral authority.

New Leadership Values

School culture, socially constructed reality, and semantic leadership are ideas compatible with the Clockworks II mindscape and with professional conceptions of teachings and teachers. Together, they provide for a leadership practice that is different from the practice of ordinary leaders.

Leadership by Purpose

Successful leaders practice leadership by purpose. Vaill (1984) defines *purposing* as "that continuous stream of actions by an organization's formal leadership which has the effect of inducing clarity, consensus and commitment regarding the organization's basic purposes" (p. 91). Bennis (1984) defines purposing as "a compelling vision of a desired state of affairs . . . which clarifies the current situation and induces commitment to the future" (p. 66).

Purposing is a powerful force because of our needs for some sense of what is important and some signal of what is of value. This force is particularly important within the context of work. We want to know what is of value, and we want a sense of order and direction; we enjoy sharing this sense with others. While many experts point out that teachers can make sense of their work lives and derive satisfaction alone, they agree that meaning, significance, and satisfaction would be considerably enhanced if this process were shared or made more public (Lortie 1975; Lieberman and Miller 1984; Rosenholtz and Kyle 1984).

When shared meaning and significance are present, people respond to work with increased motivation and commitment (Hackman and Oldham 1976). The leader's behavioral style is not as important as what the leader stands for and communicates to others. The object of purposing is the stirring of human consciousness, the enhancement of meaning, the spelling out of key cultural strands that provide both excitement and significance to our work (Sergiovanni and Starratt 1979).

Leadership by Empowerment

Highly successful leaders practice the principle of power investment: They distribute power among others in an effort to get more power in return. But their view of power investment is sophisticated; they know it is not power over people and events that counts but, rather, power over accomplishments and over the achievement of organizational purposes. To increase organizational control, they recognize that they need to delegate or surrender control over accomplishments. They understand that teachers need to be empowered to act—to be given the necessary responsibility that releases their potential and makes their actions and decisions count.

Being pragmatic, these leaders understand that management cannot function otherwise in the light of the ability-authority gap. Victor Thompson

(1961) pointed out 25 years ago that the major problem facing management was the growing gap between ability and authority. Those who have the authority to act typically don't have the necessary technical ability, and those with the ability to act typically don't have the necessary authority.

Today in teaching, and in most other fields, the gap has become more pronounced. Successful leaders recognize that leadership by empowerment can remedy this situation by lending the necessary authority to act to those with ability. But empowerment without purposing is not what is intended by this value. The two must go hand in hand. When directed and enriched by purposing and fueled by empowerment, teachers and others respond with increased motivation and commitment to work as well as surprising ability. They become smarter, using their talents more fully as they grow on the job.

Leadership as Power to Accomplish

Successful leaders know the difference between *power over* and *power to*. Power over is controlling people and events so that things turn out the way the leader wants. Thus, power over is concerned with dominance, control, and hierarchy. Leadership conceived as power over does not fit the image of schooling portrayed by the Clockworks II mindscape and the professional conceptions of the role of the teacher.

In reality, it is difficult as well as unwise to focus on programming what people do. Also, to practice leadership conceived as power over, a leader needs to be in a position of dominance, control, and hierarchy and needs to have access as well to the necessary carrots and bully sticks. But, most school leaders don't have very many carrots or bully sticks. Most leaders recognize further that people don't like this form of power and will resist it both formally and informally. Thus, even if they could use the approach, it wouldn't be very effective.

Instead, successful leaders are more concerned with the concept of *power to*. They are concerned with how the power of leadership can help people become more successful, to accomplish the things that they think are important, to experience a greater sense of efficacy. So these leaders are concerned less with what people are doing and more with what they are accomplishing.

Leadership Density

In his book, *Every Employee a Manager,* Myers (1971) observed that the more management-like jobs were, the more readily workers accepted responsibility and responded with increased motivation. Every employee a manager is a common goal among highly successful leaders because they recognize the importance of leadership density and its relationship to organizational effectiveness. Leadership density refers to the extent to which leadership roles are shared and the extent to which leadership is broadly exercised.

In highly successful schools, for example, the line between principal and teachers is not drawn very tightly, and indeed successful principals view themselves as principal-teachers. Teachers, in turn, assume a great deal of responsibility—they exercise leadership freely. The idea every teacher a leader and every principal a teacher suggests the spirit of the value of leadership density. The concept of principal teacher should not be confused with that of the instructional leader associated with the school-effectiveness movement. This latter view of the principal's role may well be associated more with the Clockworks I mindscape.

Leadership and Quality Control

Perhaps on no issue do ordinary and highly successful leaders differ more than in their beliefs about and conceptions of quality control. To ordinary leaders, quality control is a management problem that they can solve by coming up with the right controls—scheduling, prescribing, programming, monitoring, inspecting, testing, and checking. If leaders develop a system of schooling characterized by tight alignment between goals and curriculum, curriculum and teaching, teaching and testing, and if they can monitor the system with structured and standardized supervision and evaluation, then presumably they can ensure quality control.

This conception of quality control may well fit the Clockworks I mindscape and the bureaucratic conceptions of teaching, but it is not part of the Clockworks II and professional conceptions. Although successful leaders recognize that such managerial conceptions of quality control have their place, these leaders are likely to view the problem of quality control as primarily cultural rather than managerial. Quality control, they have learned, is in the minds and hearts of people at work. Quality control relates to what teachers and other school professionals believe, their commitment to quality, their sense of pride, how much they identify with their work, the ownership they feel for what they are doing, and the intrinsic satisfaction they derive from the work itself. Recognizing that the Clockworks I mindscape and the worker view of the teacher's role is dominant in American society, these successful leaders provide for a management system of quality control to avoid problems and to obtain legitimacy. On the surface, the leaders often seem to be "running a tight ship" (Meyer and Rowan 1977, Meyer 1984). But when it comes to ensuring that teaching is at its very best and that the school works as well as it can, they march to the beat of a different drummer. There is a sense in which the ways administrators talk and act are quite different (March 1984).

Leadership by Outrage

When observing highly successful school leaders at work, we see that they know the difference between sensible toughness, real toughness, and merely looking tough and acting tough. Real toughness doesn't come from flexing one's muscles simply because one happens to have more power than another. Real toughness is always principled. Successful leaders, for example, view empowerment, delegating, sharing, and other leadership values associated with the Clockworks II mindscape and professional conceptions of teaching within a target frame of reference. The eye of the target represents the core.values and beliefs of the school; the distance between this eye and the outer boundary of the target represents how these values might be articulated and implemented in the practices and work of the school.

Successful leaders expect adherence to common values but provide wide discretion in implementation. They are outraged when they see these common core values violated. The values of the common core are the non-negotiables that compose the cultural strands, the covenant that defines the way of life in the school. On the other hand, the teachers enjoy wide discretion in organizing their classrooms, deciding what to teach, and when and how, providing that the decisions they make embody the values that make up this covenant. Successful schools are both tightly and loosely structured: They are tight on values and loose on how values are embodied in the practice of teaching, supervision, and administration.

We are now at the very heart of what constitutes symbolic and cultural leadership. School cultures are concerned with the values, beliefs, and expectations that teachers, students, and others share. Cultural leaders help to shape this culture, work to design ways and means to transmit this culture to others, but more important, they behave as guardians of the values that define the culture. Key to the concept of purposing as a leadership principle, for example, is inducing clarity, consensus and commitment regarding the school's basic purposes. When teachers and students know, agree, and believe in these defining characteristics, the concept of school culture is celebrated. From these defining characteristics come not only direction but the source of meaning and significance that people find important. When the leader acts as guardian of school values, the values enjoy a special verification in importance and meaning—they become real-life cultural imperatives rather than abstractions.

The Dimensions of Cultural Leadership

The leadership theorist Robert J. House (1977) suggests that cultural leaders embody the values described above in their leadership practice by role modeling; image building; articulating and living goals, values, and purposes (the organization's covenant); exhibiting high expectations; showing confidence; and arousing motivational potential. These and other examples of cultural leadership practice are elaborated in chapters written by Terrence Deal; Robert G. Owens; David C. Dwyer, Bruce Barnett, and Ginny Lee; and

Linda T. Scheive and Marian B. Schoenheit. Many of the practices are lived by John Champlin and June E. Gabler as they write from personal experience. Confidence and expectations deserve special attention, since they are not directly examined in the discussion of leadership values above. House suggests that the combination of the leader's confidence and high expectations for others, rather than either alone, makes the difference. High expectations clarify what is important and, in the tradition of the self-fulfilling prophecy, seem able to raise others' level of commitment and performance. But when a leader espouses high expectations without at the same time communicating confidence, the expectations lose their ability to influence. Expecting more from teachers and students, for example, but then programming what they need to do by delimiting their authority and discretion communicates high expectations combined with low confidence.

A Comprehensive View of Cultural Leadership

Cultural leadership works for several reasons. From the leader's point of view, it is a pragmatic way to achieve coordinated effort toward school goals in a loosely connected world. Where management schemes fail to link together people and events in a way that provides for successful schooling, the leadership values are able to bond people together in a common cause. From an educational point of view, teaching and learning unfold best when teachers are free to make decisions that are important to them. Students in schools are best served when teachers use the system and worst served when they are subordinate to this system. From a motivational point of view, teachers and students enjoy greater satisfaction in work and respond with increased motivation when they find their work lives and activities meaningful and significant. Leadership as sense-making and the concept of school culture are the constructs for enhancing meaning and significance.

A critical connectedness exists among the various characteristics and dimensions of cultural leadership, and this concept is best understood and practiced holistically. Cultural leadership doesn't work if only some aspects are emphasized but not others. Practicing leadership by empowerment, for example, without also practicing leadership by purposing and outrage results in laissez faire rather than cultural leadership. Further, leaders who hold worker views of teachers and bureaucratic views of teaching cannot convincingly and meaning fully practice empowerment. In both cases, the rhetoric and behavior of the leader may look like the practice of empowerment conceived phonetically or in brute form, but it will not be empowerment conceived semantically or within the sense framework of followers.

Particularly fallible are attempts to adapt and practice aspects of cultural leadership while hanging on to the Clockworks I mindscape. Wholesale implementation of the school-effectiveness model[1] may well be an example of such an attempt. The literature on instructionally effective schools identifies a number of variables consistently associated with greater school "effectiveness": (1) a safe and orderly environment characterized by a sense of pride and team spirit; (2) a clear school mission and a sense of purpose; (3) high expectations for successful mastery of basic skills; (4) strong instructional leadership combined with careful and close monitoring of instruction; and (5) tight alignment between specific objectives and curriculum, curriculum and teaching, and teaching with testing. School-effectiveness experts are fond of pointing out, for example, that what gets measured gets taught.

As I review the school-effectiveness literature and study applications of this model in practice, I detect a resemblance to the Clockworks I mindscape in the rhetoric and assumptions of advocates. They seem to live in a tightly connected world. Further, though some of the variables associated with the school-effectiveness model are evidenced in the dimensions of cultural leadership (for example, variables 1 and 2 above), other variables contradict the constructs, values, and principles that characterize cultural leadership and that are found in highly successful schools (for example, variables 4 and 5 above).

Successful schools are both tightly and loosely structured. They are tightly structured with respect to basic values and sense of mission. But at the same time they allow wide discretion in how the values are to be embodied. They reflect, for example, the combined leadership values of purposing and empowerment. In successful schools, principals are less concerned with practicing close supervision that monitors what people are doing and when (leadership as power over) and more concerned with ensuring that the values of the covenant are embodied in the teachers' decisions and actions (lead-

---

[1] The language of school effectiveness has a tendency to obscure meaning. Effectiveness, for example, has both common and technical meanings. *Effective* is commonly understood to mean the ability to produce a desired effect. Thus, in a sense any school that produces effects desired by some group is considered effective by that group. But technically speaking, within educational circles, school effectiveness has taken on a specific and special meaning. An effective school is understood to be a school whose students achieve well in basic skills as measured by achievement tests. Dimensions of the school-effectiveness model have been convincingly linked to this limited view of effectiveness but not to broader, higher order, and more qualitative intellectual and academic views of effectiveness. The effective-schools model is limited by the constraints inherent in the law of conservation of information, which states that no matter how refined a model becomes or how precisely it is translated into practice, the model cannot enlarge the basic premises it rests on. The premises of the school effectiveness model are too small for it to become the template for schooling in America. For this reason I use the term *successful* to characterize schools whose effectiveness standards are more expansive and comprehensive than basic skills.

ership by outrage) and in providing help to teachers as they seek to embody those values (leadership as power to). Successful leaders do not view teachers as workers to be programmed and closely supervised but as professionals to be inspired and held accountable to shared values and commitments.

The Point of Leadership

The fallacy of displacement discussed by Thomas F. Green in chapter 8 applies here. The new leadership and understanding schools metaphorically as cultures helps us to get to the point. Within this view, we are less likely to displace the point of leadership with its technicalities. Technical and managerial conceptions of leadership have their place, but as Pat B. Guild points out in chapter 6, they should not substitute for leadership itself. In human enterprises such as the profession of teaching and schooling, technical and managerial conceptions should always be subordinate to human needs and actions and should always be practiced in service of human ends. Cultural leadership—by accepting the realities of the human spirit, by emphasizing the importance of meaning and significance, and by acknowledging the concept of professional freedom linked to values and norms that make up a moral order—comes closer to the point of leadership.

Life in schools is not exempt from the standards for judging life itself. We do not "trade in" our rights and prerogatives or commitments and responsibilities as members of life's polity to obtain school membership. Kant's (1970) principles for judging a "good polity" therefore apply to principals, supervisors, teachers, and students as they live and work together in schools:

1. The freedom of every member of society as a human being
2. The equality of each with all the others as a subject
3. The interdependence of each member of a commonwealth as a citizen (p. 74).

Freedom, equality, and interdependence and recognizing individual rights and common responsibilities of school members as human beings, subjects, and citizens provide the inner structure for school culture and are the values that cultural leadership celebrates.

References

Bennis, Warren. "Transformative Power and Leadership." In *Leadership and Organizational Culture,* edited by T.J. Sergiovanni and J.E. Corbally. Urbana: University of Illinois Press, 1984.
Bennis, Warren, and Burt Nanus. *Leaders: The Strategies for Taking Charge* . New York: Harper and Row, 1985.
Bidwell, Charles E. "The School as a Formal Organization." In *Handbook of Organizations,* edited by J.G. March. (Chicago: Rand McNally, 1965).
Burns, James McGregor. *Leadership.* New York: Harper and Row, 1978).
Cohen, Michael D., James G. March, and J. P. Olsen. "A Garbage Can Model of Organizational Choice." *Administrative Science Quarterly* 17, 1 (March 1972).

Deal, Terrence E. and Allan A. Kennedy. *Corporate Cultures: The Rites and Rituals of Corporate Life*. Reading, Mass.: Addison-Wesley, 1982.

Dwyer, David C., Ginney V. Less, Bruce G. Burnett, B.G. Filby, and Brian Rowan. *Frances Hedges and Orchard Park Elementary School: Instructional Leadership in a Stable Urban Setting*. San Francisco: Far West Lab for Educational Research and Development, 1984.

Etzioni, Amitai. *A Comparative Analysis of Complex Organizations*. New York: The Free Press, 1961.

Firestone, William A., and Bruce L. Wilson. "Using Bureaucratic and Cultural Linkages to Improve Instruction: The Principals' Contribution." *Educational Administration Quarterly* 21, 2 (1985): 7–30.

Hackman, J.R., and Greg Oldham. "Motivation Through the Design of Work: Test of a Theory." *Organizational Behavior and Human Performance* 16 (1976): 250–279.

House, Robert H. "A 1976 Theory of Charismatic Leadership." In *Leadership: The Cutting Edge,* edited by J.G. Hunt and L. Larson. Carbondale: Southern Illinois University Press, 1977.

Kant, Immanuel. "Theory and Practice." In *Kant's Political Writings,* translated by Hans Reiss. Cambridge, 1970.

Katz, F.E. "The School as a Complex Social Organization." *Harvard Educational Review* 34 (1964): 428–455.

Lieberman, Ann and Lynne Miller. *Teachers, Their World and Their Work*. Alexandria, Va.: Association for Supervision and Curriculum Development, 1984.

Lightfoot, Sara. *The Good High School: Portraits of Character and Culture*. New York: Basic Books, 1983.

Lipsitz, Joan. *Successful Schools for Young Adolescence*. New York: Transaction Press, 1983.

Lipsky, Michael. *Street-Level Bureaucracy: Dilemmas of the Individual in Public Services*. New York: Basic Books, 1980.

Lortie, Dan C. *Schoolteacher: A Sociological Study*. Chicago: University of Chicago Press, 1975.

March, James G. "How We Talk and How We Act: Administrative Theory and Administrative Life." In *Leadership and Organizational Culture,* by T.J. Sergiovanni and J.E Corbally. Urbana: University of Illinois Press, 1984.

Meyer, John W. "Organizations as Ideological Systems." In *Leadership and Organizational Culture,* edited T.J. Sergiovanni and J.E. Corbally. Urbana: University of Illinois Press, 1984.

Meyer, John W., and Brian Rowan. "Institutionalized Organization: Formal Structure as Myth and Ceremony." *American Journal of Sociology* 83 September 1977: 340–63.

Morris, Van Cleve, Robert L. Crowson, Cynthia Porter-Gehrie, and Emanuel Hurwitz, Jr. *Principals in Action: The Reality of Managing Schools*. Columbus: Charles Merrill, 1984.

Myers, Scott. *Every Employee a Manager*. New York: McGraw-Hill, 1971.

Peters, Tom and Nancy Austin. *A Passion for Excellence*. New York: Random House, 1984.

Peters, Thomas J., and Robert H. Waterman, Jr. *In Search of Excellence*. New York: Harper and Row, 1982.

Pondy, Louis R. "Leadership is a Language Game." In *Leadership: Where Else Can We Go?,* edited by M. McCall, Jr., and M.M. Lombard. Durham: Duke University Press, 1978.

Roethlisberger, Frederick, and William Dickson. *Management and the Worker*. Cambridge: Harvard University Press, 1939.

Rosenholtz, Susan J., and Susan J. Kyle, "Teacher Isolation: Barrier to Professionalism." *American Education* 8 (1984): 10–15.

Sarason, Seymour. *The Culture of the School and the Problem of Change*. Boston: Allyn and Bacon, 1971.

Schein, Edgar H. *Organizational Culture and Leadership*. San Francisco: Jossey-Bass, 1985.

Sergiovanni, Thomas J. "Ten Principles of Quality Leadership." *Educational Leadership* 39 (February 1982): 330–336.

Sergiovanni, Thomas J. "Leadership and Excellence in Schooling." *Educational Leadership* 41, 5 (February 1984): 4–14.

Sergiovanni, Thomas J. *The Principalship: A Reflective Practice Perspective*. Boston: Allyn and Bacon, 1987.

Sergiovanni, Thomas J., and Fred D. Carver. *The New School Executive: A Theory of Administration*, 2d ed. New York: Harper and Row, 1980.

Sergiovanni, Thomas J., and Robert J. Starratt. *Supervision: Human Perspectives*. New York: McGraw-Hill, 1979.

Taylor, Charles. "Interpretation and the Sciences of Man." *The Review of Metaphysics* 25 (September 1981): 3–51.

Thompson, Victor. *Modern Organizations*. New York: Knopf, 1961.

Vaill, Peter. "The Purposing of High Performing Systems." In *Leadership and Organizational Culture*, edited by T.J. Sergiovanni and J.E. Corbally. Urbana: University of Illinois Press, 1984.

Waller, Willard. *The Sociology of Teaching*. New York: John Wiley, 1967.

Weick, Karl E. "Educational Organizations as Loosely Coupled Systems." *Administrative Science Quarterly* 13, 1 (March 1976).

Weick, Karl E. "Administering Education in Loosely Coupled Schools." *Phi Delta Kappan* 27, 2 (1982): 673–676.

The Authors

Bruce G. Barnett

Project Director, Far West Laboratory for Educational Research and Development, San Francisco. Barnett has conducted and published research on effective classroom instruction. Most recently he has focused on the leadership role of the school principal by conducting research and developing inservice training programs for administrators.

John Champlin

Associate Professor, College of Education, Texas Tech University at Lubbock, Texas. During his 11 years as Superintendent of the Johnson City Schools (New York), Champlin linked mastery learning and staff development with instructional improvement. He travels nationally to consult and speak on outcome-driven program models.

Terrence E. Deal

Professor of Education, Peabody College of Vanderbilt University, Nashville, Tennessee. The study of myths, rituals and ceremonies, and symbols led to the book Deal co-authored in 1982 with Allen Kennedy, *Corporate Cultures*. His most recent book, *Modern Approaches to Understanding and Managing Organizations* (1984), continues his research emphasis on organizational culture and produces organizational results.

David C. Dwyer

Senior Educational Research Manager, Apple Computer, Inc., Cupertino, California. In his former position as Project Director at the Far West Laboratory for Educational Research and Development, Dwyer conducted research in schools with the purpose of turning new knowledge into useful practices for teachers and administrators. He has written widely and been a contributor to *Educational Leadership.*

June E. Gabler

Superintendent, Fort Dodge Community School District, Fort Dodge, Iowa. Gabler was 1986 President of the American Association of School Administrators, a member of the U.S. Congressional Commission on Funding of Education for Special Needs Children, and a member of the Board of the Institute of School Executives.

Thomas F. Green
Margaret Slocum Professor of Education and Philosophy, Syracuse University, Syracuse, New York. Green delivered the 1984 John Dewey Lecture on "The Formation of Conscience in an Age of Technology." He was distinguished lecturer, Kyoto American Studies Seminar, Kyoto, Japan, in 1985. His primary interest is in educational issues of public policy and ethics. His current theme is the voices of conscience.

Pat Burke Guild
President, Pat Guild Associates, Seattle, Washington. Guild is coordinator of the Learning Styles Programs at Seattle Pacific University, where she also serves as a graduate faculty member. She co-authored with Stephen Garger the 1985 ASCD publication, *Marching to Different Drummers.*

Ginny V. Lee
Associate Research Scientist, Far West Laboratory for Educational Research and Development, San Francisco. Lee is currently conducting research in a national study of students' instructional experiences in Chapter I programs and designing and refining training and inservice in the Peer Assisted Leadership Program (PAL).

Robert G. Owens
Distinguished Research Professor, Department of Administration and Policy Studies, Hofstra University, Hempstead, New York. Owens' research interest in organizational development and theory is reflected in writing and lectures. He is author of *Organizational Behavior in Education* (3d ed., 1987) and "Methodological Rigor in Naturalistic Inquiry: Some Issues and Answers," which appeared in *Educational Administration Quarterly* (1982). He co-authored *Administering Change in Education* (1976).

Marian Beauchamp Schoenheit, co-editor
Director, Elementary Education, Liverpool Central School District, Liverpool, New York. Schoenheit is a former principal of elementary and junior high schools. She has taught educational administration and curriculum courses at the University of the State of New York at Oswego, Syracuse University, and Utica College.

Thomas J. Sergiovanni
Lillian Radford Professor of Education, Trinity University, San Antonio, Texas. Sergiovanni is author of several books, including *Supervision Human Perspectives* (3d ed., 1983) and Handbook for Effective Department Leadership (2d ed., 1984). His most recent work is *The Principalship: A Reflective Practice Perspective* (1986).

Linda Tinelli Sheive, co-editor

Chair, Department of Educational Administration, State University of New York College at Oswego. During the development of the 1987 ASCD Yearbook, Sheive was Assistant Professor of Educational Administration at Syracuse University, Syracuse, New York. Her field-based research on organizational literacy, the school as a workplace, and the school as a setting for teacher and administrator learning is the basis for her writing and consulting.

Reactor Panel

Three groups assisted in the development of the yearbook: the ASCD Publications Committee, ASCD members, and students in an educational administration program.

The following ASCD members served as a reactor panel at the 1986 ASCD conference in San Francisco, California.

- Doug Gowler, Principal, Sagebrush Elementary School, Cherry Creek School District, Aurora, Colorado. Gowler has served on the Standards Committee, National Association of Elementary Principals, and has contributed to Standards of Quality Elementary Schools, K-8 (1984) and Proficiencies for Principals K-8 (1986).
- Helen McIntyre, Principal, Shorewood High School, Shoreline School District #412, Seattle, Washington. McIntyre's published works include "The First Year Principal," *National Association of Secondary School Principals Bulletin* (1985).
- Nelson W. "Pete" Quinby, III, Director of Secondary Education, Regional District No. 9, Joel Barlow High School, West Redding, Connecticut. Quinby's contributions to *Educational Leadership* (1985) include "Improving the Place Called School: A Conversation with John Goodlad" and "On Testing and Teaching Intelligence: A Conversation with Robert Sternberg."

Members of a Seminar in Educational Leadership, Syracuse University, Syracuse, New York, participated in discussions about yearbook chapters. They were:

- Constance Busch, Principal, House IV, Liverpool High School, Liverpool, New York
- Katherine A. M. Carlson, Director, Pupil Personnel Services, Skaneateles Central School District, Skaneateles, New York
- Jeanne Logan, Assistant Principal, Ray Middle School, Baldwinsville Central School District, Baldwinsville, New York
- Eva Shapiro, Instructional Supervisor, Baldwinsville Central School District, Baldwinsville, New York
- Samuel Shevat, Principal, Canton High School, Canton, New York
- David Wheeler, Principal, Wellwood Middle School, Fayetteville-Manlius Central School District, Fayetteville, New York

ASCD

Board of Directors as of November 1, 1986

Executive Council 1986-87

President: Gerald Firth, Professor and Chair, Department of Curriculum and Supervision, University of Georgia, Athens.

President-Elect: Marcia Knoll, Director of Curriculum and Instruction, District 28–Queens, Forest Hills, New York.

Immediate Past President: Carolyn Sue Hughes, Assistant Superintendent, Oklahoma City Public Schools, Oklahoma City, Oklahoma.

Roger V. Bennett, Dean, College of Education and Allied Professions, Bowling Green State University, Bowling Green, Ohio.

Donna Jean Carter, Superintendent, Independent School District 281, New Hope, Minnesota.

Denice S. Clyne, Principal, Sand Lake School, Anchorage, Alaska.

Patricia C. Conran, Superintendent, Bexley City Schools, Bexley, Ohio.

Robert C. Hanes, Deputy Superintendent of Schools, Charlotte-Mecklenburg Schools, Charlotte, North Carolina.

Corrine P. Hill, Principal, Wasatch Elementary School, Salt Lake City, Utah.

Anna Jolivet, Director of Planning Services, Tucson Unified School District, Tucson, Arizona.

Jean V. Marani, Supervisor, Early Childhood and Elementary Education, Florida Department of Education, Tallahassee.

Stephanie A. Marshall, Director, Illinois Math & Science Academy, Aurora, Illinois.

Loren E. Sanchez, Associate Superintendent of Instruction, Upland School District, Upland, California.

Board Members Elected at Large

(Listed alphabetically; the year in parentheses indicates the end of the term of office.)

Doris Brown, University of Missouri, St. Louis (1987).

Rita Foote, Southfield Public Schools, Southfield, Michigan (1989).

Geneva Gay, Purdue University, West Lafayette, Indiana (1987).

Delores Greene, Richmond Public Schools, Richmond, Virginia (1988).

Evelyn B. Holman, Wicomico County Board of Education, Salisbury, Maryland (1990).

Robert Krajewski, University of Texas, San Antonio (1989).

Richard Kunkel, National Council for Accreditation of Teacher Education, Washington, D.C. (1988).

Blanche J. Martin, E.S.R. Winnebago/Boone Counties, Rockford, Illinois (1990).

Lillian Ramos, Catholic University, Ponce, Puerto Rico (1989).

Arthur D. Roberts, University of Connecticut, Storrs (1987).

Thelma Spencer, Educational Testing Services, Princeton, New Jersey (1989).

Arthur Steller, Oklahoma City Public Schools, Oklahoma City, Oklahoma (1987).

Roberta Walker, D.C. Public Schools, Washington, D.C. (1990).

Lois F. Wilson, California State University, San Bernardino (1988).

Marilyn Winters, Sacramento State University, Sacramento, California (1990).

George Woons, Kent Intermediate School District, Grand Rapids, Michigan (1989).

Claire Yoshida, Naalehu High School, Keala Kekua, Hawaii (1988).

Unit Representatives to the Board of Directors

(Each unit's President is listed first.)

Alabama: Carl W. Ponder, Talladega County Schools, Talladega; Horace Gordon, Birmingham; Richard Brogdon, Auburn University, Auburn.

Alaska: Alice J. Bosshard, Valdez City Schools, Valdez; M. Denice Clyne, Sand Lake School, Anchorage

Arizona: Peg Moseley, Peoria Unified School District, Peoria; Ellie Sbragia, Arizona Bar Foundation, Phoenix.

Arkansas: Beverly C. Reed, Siloam Springs Public Schools, Siloam Springs; Jerry Daniel, Camden Public Schools, Camden.

California: Loren Sanchez, Upland School District, Upland; Ronald Hockwalt, Cajon Valley High School District, El Cajon; Marilyn George, Kern Union High School District, Bakersfield; Bob Guerts, Sonoma Valley Unified School District, Santa Rosa; Yvonne Lux, Poway Unified School District, Poway; Dolores Ballesteros, Franklin-McKinley Elementary School District, San Jose; Dorothy Garcia, Zimmerman School, Bloomington; Bob Garrison, California State University, Sacramento.

Colorado: Mary R. Leiker, St. Vrain Valley School District, Longmont; Mel Preusser, Castle Rock; Gary Gibson, Adams County School District #14, Commerce City.

Connecticut: Tom Jokubaitis, Wolcott Public Schools, Wolcott; Edward H. Bourque, Fairfield Public Schools, Fairfield; Roberta Ohotnicky, Regional School District #16, Prospect.

Delaware: Ethel Hines, Adminstrative Office, Newark; Frederick Duffy, Lincoln.

District of Columbia: Delores C. Carter, D.C. Public Schools, Washington, D.C.; Romaine Thomas, Ketcham Elementary School, Washington, D.C.

Florida: F. Virgil Mills, School Board of Manatee County, Bradenton; Mary Jo Sisson, Okaloosa District Schools, Ft. Walton Beach; Eileen Duval, Gifted and Talented Programs, Elementary Education, Tampa.

Georgia: Charles Shepherd, Georgia Department of Education, Calhoun; Priscilla Doster, Monroe County Schools, Forsyth; Wilma Biggers, Oconee County Schools, Watkinsville.

Hawaii: Leslie H. Correa, St. Louis High School, Honolulu; Donald Young, Kailua.

Idaho: Linda Clark, Joplin Elementary School, Boise; Lamont Lyons, Boise.

Illinois: James Montgomery, Arlington Heights Public Schools, Arlington Heights; John Fletcher, Park Ridge School District #64, Park Ridge; Sheila Wilson, Forest View Educational Center, Arlington Heights; Al Cohen, Wilmot Junior High School, Deerfield; Carolyn S. Kimbell, Downers Grove School District #58, Downers Grove; Richard Hanke, Thomas Junior High School, Arlington Heights.

Indiana: David G. Ebeling, Monroe County Community School Corporation, Bloomington; Sue Pifer, Bartholomew Community School Corporation, Columbus; Sam Abram, Muncie Community Schools, Muncie.·

Iowa: Morris D. Wilson, Des Moines Public Schools, Des Moines; Douglas G. Schermer, Briggs Elementary School, Maquoketa; Arnold N. Lindaman, North Scott Community School District, Eldridge.

Kansas: Helen Hooper, Salina Unified School District #305, Salina; Tom Hawk, Unified School District #383, Manhattan; Jim Jarrett, Unified School District #588, Kansas City.

Kentucky: Linda Cline, Allen County Board of Education, Scottsville.

Louisiana: Constance C. Dolese, Orleans Parish School Board, New Orleans; Julianna Boudreaux, Area II Elementary Schools, New Orleans; Mary Kate Scully, Area II Elementary Schools, New Orleans.

Maine: Joanne Lebel, Martel School, Lewiston; Lawrence Frazier, Woolwich Central School, Woolwich; Scott Myers, Nezinscot Valley School District, Buckfield.

Maryland: Tom Howie, Huntingtown Elementary School, Huntingtown; Joan Palmer, Howard County Public Schools, Ellicott City; Richard Williams, Towson State University, Towson.

Massachusetts: Gary G. Baker, Acton-Boxborough Region Schools, Acton-Boxborough; Peter Farrelly, Wachusett Regional School District, Holden;

Therese d'Abre, Dennis-Yarmouth Regional Schools, South Yarmouth; Isa Zimmerman, Lexington Public Schools, Lexington.

Michigan: Marilyn Van Valkenburgh, East Grand Rapids Schools, Grand Rapids; Sam Mangione, Wayne County Intermediate School District, Wayne; Lenore Croudy, Flint; Ronald Sergeant, Kalamazoo Valley Intermediate School District, Kalamazoo; Charles King, Michigan Education Association, East Lansing.

Minnesota: Jerry Spies, Jordan Secondary School, Jordan; Merill Fellger, Buffalo Public Schools, Buffalo; Karen Johnson, Oakdale Public Schools, Maplewood.

Mississippi: Dwight Shelton, Pascagoula Municipal Schools, Pascagoula; Tommye Henderson, West Point School District, West Point.

Missouri: Charles Brown, Hickman Mills School District, Harrisonville; Anne E. Price, St. Louis Public Schools, St. Louis; Cameron Pulliam, Mark Twain Elementary School, Brentwood.

Montana: John Dracon, Billings Public Schools, Billings; Louise Bell, Eastern Montana College, Billings.

Nebraska: Susan Spangler, Millard Public Schools, Omaha; L. James Walter, University of Nebraska, Lincoln; Ron Reichert, Sydney Public Schools, Sydney.

Nevada: Monte Littell, Clark County School District, Las Vegas; Jerry Conner, Nevada Association of School Administrators, Las Vegas.

New Hampshire: Jean Stefanik, Wilkins School, Amherst; Carl Wood, Greenland Central School, Greenland.

New Jersey: Fred Young, Hamilton Township Schools, Hamilton; Judith Zimmerman, Constable School, Kendall Park; Paul Lempa, Bayonne School District, Bayonne; Paul Manko, Hattie Britt School, Mt. Laurel Township; Thomas Lubben, Englewood Board of Education, Englewood.

New Mexico: Marguarite Ballmer, Cobre Consolidated Schools, Bayard; Bettye M. Coffey, Ernie Pyle Middle School, Albuquerque.

New York: Nicholas F. Vitalo, Jr., Malloy College, Rockville Center; Florence Seldin, Pittsford Central Schools, Pittsford; Donald E. Harkness, Manhasset Union Free School District, Manhasset; Donna Moss, South Seneca Central School, Interlaken; Arlene B. Soifer, Nassau BOCES, Carle Place; Timothy M. Melchior, Memorial Junior High School, Valley Stream; Judith Johnson, Nyack Public Schools, Nyack; Sam Alessi, Jr., Buffalo.

North Carolina: Charles P. Bentley, Northwest Regional Education Center, North Wilkesboro; Don Lassiter, Nash County Schools, Nashville; Marcus Smith, Salisbury City Schools, Salisbury.

North Dakota: Ron Stammen, Divide County Public Schools, Crosby; Andy Keough, North Dakota State University, Fargo.

Ohio: David Kirkton, Westlake City Schools, Westlake; Eugene G. Glick, Seville; Roger Coy, Beavercreek Local Schools, Beavercreek; Irma Lou

Griggs, Lake Local Schools, Hartville; Larry Zimmerman, Marysville Exempted Village Schools, Marysville.

Oklahoma: Charles Dodson, Sapulpa Public Schools, Sapulpa; Tom Gallaher, Oklahoma University, Norman; James Roberts, Lawton Public Schools, Lawton.

Oregon: Gerald Scovil, North Clackamas School District, Milwaukee; Thomas S. Lindersmith, Lake Oswego; LaVae Robertson, Oak Elementary School, Albany.

Pennsylvania: John T. Lambert, East Stroudsburg Area School District, East Stroudsburg; John P. Jarvie, Northwest Tri-County Intermediate Unit #5, Edinboro; John T. Lambert, Administration Center, East Stroudsburg; Ina Logue, Allegheny Intermediate Unit, Pittsburgh; Donald Wright, Montgomery County Intermediate Unit, Erdenheim.

Puerto Rico: Jannette Gavillan, University of Puerto Rico, Bayamon; Ramon Claudio Tirado, University of Puerto Rico, Rio Piedras.

South Carolina: Louise M. Weekes, Spartanburg School District 6, Spartanburg; Milton Kimpson, South Carolina Industrial Commission, Columbia; Karen B. Callison, Union County Schools, Union.

South Dakota: Dan Brosz, Huron Public Schools, Huron; Donlynn Rice, Pierre.

Tennessee: Kay Awalt, Franklin Elementary School, Franklin; Betty Sparks, State Department of Education, Knoxville; Cindy Chance, Milan Special School District, Milan.

Texas: Charles Patterson, Killeen Independent School District, Killeen; Pat Mengwasser, Texas Education Agency, Austin; Genevieve Mandina, Sam Houston State University, Huntsville; Margaret Montgomery, Tyler Independent School District, Tyler; Bonnie Fairall, El Paso Independent School District, El Paso; Nancy Barker, Carrollton-Farmers Branch Independent School District, Carrollton.

Utah: Merrell Hanson, Provo School District, Provo; Peggy Sorenson, East Sandy School, Sandy.

Vermont: Suzanne Bryant Armstrong, Franklin Central Supervisory Union, St. Albans; Lynn Baker Murray, Trinity College, Burlington.

Virginia: Katherine Rodgers, York County Public Schools, Grafton; Evelyn Bickham, Lynchburg College, Lynchburg; Shelba Murphy, Alexandria; Marion Hargrove, Bedford County Public Schools, Bedford.

Virgin Islands: Yegin Habteyes, St. Thomas; Anita Plasket, College of the Virgin Islands, St. Croix.

Washington: Jim Barchek, Kent School District, Kent; Bob Valiant, Kennewick School District, Kennewick; Monica Schmidt, State Board of Education, Olympia.

West Virginia: Robert Mason, Mineral County Schools, Keyser; Corey Lock, Marshall University, Huntington.

Wisconsin: Sherwood Williams, Ashwaubenon Schools, Green Bay; John Koehn, Oconomowoc Area School District, Oconomowoc; Arnold M. Chandler, Bureau for Program Development, Madison.

Wyoming: Marc McClanahan, Crook County District I, Sundance; Donna Connor, University of Wyoming, Rawlins.

International Units:

British Columbia: Donna Greenstreet, Winslow Centre, Coquitlam.

Germany: Richard A. Penkava, Department of Defense Dependents Schools.

United Kingdom: Sydney Elstran, Department of Defense Dependents Schools.

ASCD Review Council

Chair: J. Arch Phillips, Kent State University, Kent, Ohio.
Donna Delph, Purdue University Calumet, Hammond, Indiana.
Nelson "Pete" Quinby, Joel Barlow High School, West Redding, Connecticut.
Barbara D. Day, University of North Carolina, Chapel Hill, North Carolina.
Dolores Silva, Temple University, Philadelphia, Pennsylvania

ASCD Headquarters Staff

Gordon Cawelti, *Executive Director*
Ronald S. Brandt, *Executive Editor*
John Bralove, *Director, Administrative Services*
Diane Berreth, *Director, Field Services*
Helené Hodges, *Director, Research and Information*
Lewis Rhodes, *Manager, Media and Technology*
Cynthia Warger, *Director, Program Development*

Sarah Arlington
Sylvia Bayer
Barbara Beach
Karla Bingman
Elizabeth Blaize
Joan Brandt
Dorothy Brown
Kathy Browne
Colette Burgess
Raiza Chernault
Fran Cohen
Kathy Compton
Marcia D'Arcangelo
Lois Davis
Marsha Davis
Pam Dronka
Anita Fitzpatrick
Glenda Fountain
Janet Frymoyer
Valerie Grande
Dorothy Haines

Susan Hartsoe
Sandy Hightower
Nina Hillary
Mary Hines
Harold Hutch
Consuella Jenkins
Debbie Johnson
Jo Ann Jones
Teola Jones
Michelle Kelly
Donna Lands
Amy Lashbrook
Indu Madan
Debbie Maddox
Gary Maxwell
Anjanette McMillan
Clara Meredith
Frances Mindel
Ricky Mitchell
Nancy Modrak
Cerylle Fritts Moffett

Kelvin Parnell
Margini Patel
Jackie Porter
Ruby Powell
Lorraine Primeau
Gayle Rockwell
Nancy Schroer
Bob Shannon
Carolyn Shell
Leslie Shell
Chris Smith
Lisa Street
Dee Stump-Walek
René Townsley
Liz Trexler
Mary Tyrrell
Al Way
Cheryl Weber
Sylvia Wisnom